THE TECHNOLOGICAL
SINGULARITY

D0954856

The MIT Press Essential Knowledge Series

NOV 1 8 2015

THE TECHNOLOGICAL SINGULARITY

MURRAY SHANAHAN

The MIT Press | Cambridge, Massachusetts | London, England

© 2015 Massachusetts Institute of Technology

All rights reserved. No part of this book may be reproduced in any form by any electronic or mechanical means (including photocopying, recording, or information storage and retrieval) without permission in writing from the publisher.

MIT Press books may be purchased at special quantity discounts for business or sales promotional use. For information, please email special_sales@mitpress.mit.edu

This book was set in Chaparral by the MIT Press. Printed and bound in the United States of America.

Library of Congress Cataloging-in-Publication Data

Shanahan, Murray.
The technological singularity / Murray Shanahan.
    pages   cm
Includes bibliographical references and index.
ISBN 978-0-262-52780-4 (pbk. : alk. paper)
1. Artificial intelligence—Forecasting. 2. Artificial intelligence—Psychological aspects. 3. Technology—Social aspects. 4. Conscious automata. 5. Brain—Computer simulation. I. Title.
Q335.S4626 2015
006.3—dc23

                                                                    2015000997

10 9 8 7 6 5 4 3 2 1

These remarks might appear fanciful to some readers, but to the writer they seem very real and urgent, and worthy of emphasis outside of science fiction.

I. J.Good, *Speculations Concerning the First Ultraintelligent Machine* (1965)

Real motive problem, with an AI. Not human, see?

William Gibson, *Neuromancer* (1984)

CONTENTS

SERIES FOREWORD

The MIT Press Essential Knowledge series offers accessible, concise, beautifully produced pocket-size books on topics of current interest. Written by leading thinkers, the books in this series deliver expert overviews of subjects that range from the cultural and the historical to the scientific and the technical.

In today's era of instant information gratification, we have ready access to opinions, rationalizations, and superficial descriptions. Much harder to come by is the foundational knowledge that informs a principled understanding of the world. Essential Knowledge books fill that need. Synthesizing specialized subject matter for nonspecialists and engaging critical topics through fundamentals, each of these compact volumes offers readers a point of access to complex ideas.

Bruce Tidor
Professor of Biological Engineering and Computer Science
Massachusetts Institute of Technology

PREFACE

Like many others who have dedicated their working lives to research in artificial intelligence, I was inspired as a child by science fiction. My boyhood hero was not a real person. It was Susan Calvin, the scientist in Asimov's *I Robot* stories (the written works, not the film) who pioneered the field of robot psychology. More than anyone else, I wanted to be like her when I grew up. Now that I have (sort of) grown up, and in real life bear the title of Professor of Cognitive Robotics, I have a more complex relationship with science fiction. I still see it as a source of inspiration and as a medium for exploring important philosophical ideas. However, the ideas it explores merit a deeper treatment. The primary purpose of science fiction is to entertain, albeit in an intellectually stimulating way. It would be a mistake to use it as a guide to thinking.

So this is not intended as a work of science fiction. Nor is it a piece of so-called futurology. The aim here is not to make predictions. Rather, it is to investigate a range of possible future scenarios, without committing to the prospect of any one in particular, and without any particular timescale in mind. Indeed even highly unlikely or remote scenarios are sometimes worthy of study. This is true, for instance, if a scenario is especially dystopian. In that case we might want to think carefully about how to reduce its likelihood even further. Unlikely or remote scenarios are also worth discussing if they raise interesting philosophical questions, obliging us, for example, to think about what we really want as a species. So whether or not you think we will soon create human-level artificial intelligence, whether or not you think the singularity is near, the very idea deserves some serious thought.

This is a short book on a very large theme. So it can only stand as an introduction, with many important issues given only a brief treatment. For example, various arguments relating to consciousness are presented to which there are well-known counterarguments, and these merit counterarguments of their own. But an introductory book has to skip over these subtleties. Also the focus is heavily on the future of artificial intelligence, and some significant related topics, such as nanotechnology and biotechnology, are barely touched on. The book is intended to provide a neutral overview of the conceptual territory, and I have attempted to outline both sides of the argument in controversial matters. However, it seems unavoidable that some of my own views will be visible through the veil of neutrality, despite my best efforts.

I would like to thank the very many people who have discussed artificial intelligence with me over the decades, not only academics and students but also members of the public who have attended my talks. I would like to thank them all by name, but that would be impossible. So I will reserve my explicit gratitude for a few colleagues whose recent influence has been especially pertinent. Thanks to Stuart Armstrong, Nick Bostrom, Andrew Davison, Daniel Dewey, Randal Koene, Richard Newcombe, Owen Holland, Huw Price, Stuart Russell, Anders Sandberg, and Jaan Tallinn. Sorry to those I have forgotten. Finally, I would like to thank MIT Press, and especially Bob Prior, for encouraging me to write the book in the first place.

Murray Shanahan
North Norfolk and South Kensington, October 2014

INTRODUCTION

In recent years the idea that human history is approaching a "singularity" thanks to increasingly rapid technological advance has moved from the realm of science fiction into the sphere of serious debate. In physics, a singularity is a point in space or time, such as the center of a black hole or the instant of the Big Bang, where mathematics breaks down and our capacity for comprehension along with it. By analogy, a singularity in human history would occur if exponential technological progress brought about such dramatic change that human affairs as we understand them today came to an end.[1] The institutions we take for granted—the economy, the government, the law, the state—these would not survive in their present form. The most basic human values—the sanctity of life, the pursuit of happiness, the freedom to choose—these would be superseded. Our very understanding of what it means to be human—to be an individual, to be alive, to be conscious, to be part of the social order—all this would be thrown into question, not by detached philosophical reflection, but through force of circumstances, real and present.

What kind of technological progress could possibly bring about such upheaval? The hypothesis we will examine in this book is that a technological singularity of this sort could be precipitated by significant advances in either (or both) of two related fields: artificial intelligence (AI) and neurotechnology. Already we know how to tinker with the stuff of life, with genes and DNA. The ramifications of biotechnology are large enough, but they are dwarfed by the potential ramifications of learning how to engineer the "stuff of mind."

Today the intellect is, in an important sense, fixed, and this limits both the scope and pace of technological advance. Of course the store of human knowledge has been increasing for millennia, and our ability to disseminate that knowledge has increased along with it, thanks to writing, printing, and the Internet. Yet the organ that produces knowledge, the brain of *homo sapiens*, has remained fundamentally unchanged throughout the same period, its cognitive prowess unrivalled.

This will change if the fields of artificial intelligence and neurotechnology fulfill their promise. If the intellect becomes, not only the producer, but also a product of technology, then a feedback cycle with unpredictable and potentially explosive consequences can result. For when the thing being engineered is intelligence itself, the very thing doing the engineering, it can set to work improving itself. Before long, according to the singularity hypothesis, the ordinary human is removed from the loop, overtaken by artificially intelligent machines or by cognitively enhanced biological intelligence and unable to keep pace.

When the thing being engineered is intelligence itself, the very thing doing the engineering, it can set to work improving itself.

Does the singularity hypothesis deserve to be taken seriously, or is it just an imaginative fiction? One argument for taking it seriously is based on what Ray Kurzweil calls the *"law of accelerating returns."* An area of technology is subject to the law of accelerating returns if the rate at which the technology improves is proportional to how good the technology is. In other words, the better the technology is, the faster it gets better, yielding exponential improvement over time.

A prominent example of this phenomenon is Moore's law, according to which the number of transistors that can be fabricated on a single chip doubles every eighteen months or so.[2] Remarkably, the semiconductor industry has managed to adhere to Moore's law for several decades. Other indexes of progress in information technology, such as CPU clock speed and network bandwidth, have followed similar exponential curves. But information technology isn't the only area where we see accelerating progress. In medicine, for example, DNA sequencing has fallen exponentially in cost while increasing exponentially in speed, and the technology of brain scanning has enjoyed an exponential increase in resolution.[3]

On a historical timescale, these accelerating trends can be seen in the context of a series of technological landmarks occurring at ever-decreasing intervals: agriculture, printing, electric power, the computer. On an even longer, evolutionary timescale, this technological series was itself preceded by a sequence of evolutionary milestones that also arose at ever-decreasing intervals: eukaryotes, vertebrates, primates, *homo sapiens*. These facts have led some commentators to view the human race as riding on a curve of dramatically increasing complexity that stretches into the distant past. Be that as it may, we need only extrapolate the technological portion of the curve a little way into the future to reach an important tipping point, the point at which human technology renders the ordinary human technologically obsolete.[4]

Of course, every exponential technological trend must reach a plateau eventually, thanks to the laws of physics, and there are any number of economic, political, or scientific reasons why an exponential trend might stall before reaching its theoretical limit. But let us suppose that the technological trends most relevant to AI and neurotechnology maintain their accelerating momentum, precipitating the ability to engineer the stuff of mind, to synthesize and manipulate the very machinery of intelligence. At this point, intelligence itself, whether artificial or human, would become subject to the law of accelerating returns, and from here to a technological singularity is but a small leap of faith.

Some authors confidently predict that this watershed will occur in the middle of the 21st century. But there are other reasons for thinking through the idea of the singularity than prophecy, which anyway is a hit-and-miss affair. First, the mere concept is profoundly interesting from an intellectual standpoint, regardless of when or even whether it comes about. Second, the very possibility, however remote it might seem, merits discussion today on purely pragmatic, strictly rational grounds. Even if the arguments of the futurists are flawed, we need only assign a small probability to the anticipated event for it to command our most sincere attention. For the consequences for humanity, if a technological singularity did indeed occur, would be seismic.

What are these potentially seismic consequences? What sort of world, what sort of universe, might come into being if a technological singularity does occur? Should we fear the prospect of the singularity, or should we welcome it? What, if anything, can we do today or in the near future to secure the best possible outcome? These are chief among the questions to be addressed in the coming pages. They are large questions. But the prospect, even just the concept, of the singularity promises to shed new light on ancient philosophical questions that are perhaps even larger. What is the essence of our humanity? What are our most fundamental values? How should we live? What, in all this, are we willing to give up? For the possibility of a technological singularity poses both an existential risk and an existential opportunity.

It poses an existential risk in that it potentially threatens the very survival of the human species. This may sound like hyperbole, but today's emerging technologies have a potency never before seen. It isn't hard to believe that a highly contagious, drug-resistant virus could be genetically engineered with sufficient morbidity to bring about such a catastrophe. Only a lunatic would create such a thing deliberately. But it might require little more than foolishness to engineer a virus capable of mutating into such a monster. The reasons why advanced AI poses an existential risk are analogous, but far more subtle. We will explore these in due course. In the meantime suffice to say that it is only rational to consider the future possibility of some corporation, government, organization, or even some individual, creating and then losing control of an exponentially self-improving, resource-hungry artificial intelligence.

On a more optimistic note, a technological singularity could also be seen as an existential opportunity, in the more philosophical sense of the word "existential." The capability to engineer the stuff of mind opens up the possibility of transcending our biological heritage and thereby overcoming its attendant limitations. Foremost among these limitations is mortality. An animal's body is a fragile thing, vulnerable to disease, damage, and decay, and the biological brain, on which human consciousness (today) depends, is merely one of its parts. But if we acquire the means to repair any level of damage to it, and ultimately to rebuild it from scratch, possibly in a nonbiological substrate, then there is nothing to preclude the unlimited extension of consciousness.

Life extension is one facet of a trend in thought known as "transhumanism". But why should we be satisfied with human life as we know it? If we can rebuild the brain, why should we not also be able to redesign it, to upgrade it? (The same question might be asked about the human body, but our concern here is the intellect.) Conservative improvements in memory, learning, and attention are achievable by pharmaceutical means. But the ability to re-engineer the brain from bottom to top suggests the possibility of more radical forms of cognitive enhancement and re-organization. What could or should we do with such transformative powers? At least, so one argument goes, it would mitigate the existential risk posed by superintelligent machines. It would allow us to keep up, although we might change beyond all recognition in the process.

The largest, and most provocative, sense in which a technological singularity might be an existential opportunity can only be grasped by stepping outside the human perspective altogether and adopting a more cosmological point of view. It is surely the height of anthropocentric thinking to suppose that the story of matter in this corner of the universe climaxes with human society and the myriad living brains embedded in it, marvelous as they are. Perhaps matter still has a long way to go on the scale of complexity. Perhaps there are forms of consciousness yet to arise that are, in some sense, superior to our own. Should we recoil from this prospect, or rejoice in it? Can we even make sense of such an idea? Whether or not the singularity is near, these are questions worth asking, not least because in attempting to answer them we shed new light on ourselves and our place in the order of things.

ROUTES TO ARTIFICIAL INTELLIGENCE

1.1 Artificial General Intelligence

In 1950 the wartime code-breaker and computing pioneer Alan Turing published a paper in the journal *Mind* entitled "Computing Machinery and Intelligence."[1] It was the first serious, scholarly treatment of the concept of artificial intelligence. Turing predicted that by the year 2000 people would "be able to speak of machines thinking without expecting to be contradicted." He envisaged that machines would be able to pass what has become known as the *Turing Test*.

The Turing Test involves a kind of game. Two "players," one human and the other a machine, communicate with another person, the "judge," through a keyboard and screen. The judge holds a conversation with each of the players in turn, and tries to guess which is the human and which is the machine. The task for the machine is to convince the judge that it is the human—a feat, so the argument goes, that would surely require human-level intelligence. If the judge is unable to tell human from machine, then the machine has passed the test. Writing in 1950, Turing anticipated a world in which machines capable of passing his test were commonplace, a world in which "thinking machines" were familiar, in the home and in the workplace.

Despite Turing's prediction, human-level AI had not been achieved by the year 2000, nor was there any sign that it might be around the corner. No machine could come close to passing the Turing Test. Nevertheless, one significant milestone in artificial intelligence had recently been attained. In 1997 Deep Blue, a computer developed by IBM, defeated then world chess champion Garry Kasparov. In contrast to previous chess programs he had beaten, which to him seemed predictable and mechanical, Kasparov allegedly said he sensed an "alien intelligence" on the other side of the board when he played against Deep Blue.[2]

It's instructive to stand back and ponder this moment in the history of AI. The field had accomplished something that half a century beforehand might have been considered its crowning achievement. Humanity had been outstripped by a machine. Of course, a car can move faster than the fastest human sprinter, and a crane can hoist far more than a champion weight-lifter. But intellectual prowess is what sets human beings apart from the rest of the animals, and chess is a quintessentially intellectual pursuit.

Now computer chess was cracked. Yet somehow we seemed no nearer to human-level AI than in Turing's time. How could this be? The problem with Deep Blue was that it was a specialist. All it could do was play chess. Contrast this with a typical human adult. Take the office worker who has just walked past the window of the café where I am sitting with my laptop. Her day has no doubt been a busy patchwork of activities—making a packed lunch, reviewing the children's homework, driving to work, composing emails, fixing the photocopier, and so on. Each of these activities, examined more closely, requires the exercise of multiple sensorimotor skills. Consider the task of making a packed lunch. This involves retrieving utensils and ingredients from various places, opening packets, chopping, cutting, spreading, and so on.

In short, a human being is a generalist, a jack of all trades. A human chess champion can do a whole lot more than just play chess. Moreover a human being is adaptive. Fixing photocopiers is not an innate capability. It is learned. Had the office worker been born in a different century or a different culture, she would have acquired a different set of skills. And if she has the misfortune to lose her present job, she can re-train for another one. The achievements of AI research in a variety of specialist domains (chess being just one among many success stories) contrast starkly with the field's failure to produce a machine with general purpose, adaptive intelligence. So how could we produce *artificial general intelligence*? Before we can speculate in an informed way about machine superintelligence, we need to answer this question.[3]

An essential feature of biological intelligence is *embodiment*. Unlike Deep Blue, a human being is an animal with a body, and its brain is part of that body. The brain of an animal has evolved to maintain the well-being of that body and to perpetuate the genes that it carries. The body has muscles, enabling it to move, and senses, so that its movements can be made to depend on the state of the environment, the better to subserve its mission. The brain sits in the middle of this sensorimotor loop, shaping the animal's actions according to what it perceives. Human intelligence, for all its glorious achievements, is fundamentally an extension of animal intelligence, and the human capacities for language, reason, and creativity all rest on a sensorimotor foundation.

So while the endeavor to create artificial general intelligence might do away with much that is essential to biological life, such as metabolism and reproduction, perhaps embodiment is a methodological necessity. Perhaps the need to engage with a messy, dynamic, physical environment full of complex and varied objects, both animate and inanimate, is at the root of intelligence. The Turing Test is a poor benchmark, in this light, since it involves only language. The only way to form a reliable judgment of the intelligence of an artifact is to observe its behavior in an environment like our own. And the only way to achieve human-level AI, according to this way of thinking, is through robotics. Later we will examine challenges to this principle of embodiment. But let's adopt it for the time being. Our basic question can then be reformulated. How can we endow a robot with general intelligence?

Perhaps general intelligence is simply the sum of many specialist sensorimotor skills, and the problem is simply that AI hasn't yet replicated enough of them. When robots have been given a certain critical mass of skills, general intelligence will somehow emerge. Well, even if we gloss over the many engineering questions this proposal begs, it remains unconvincing. The products of such an approach might briefly give the appearance of general intelligence. But nobody would be fooled for very long. The multi-specialist is going to get stuck as soon as it has to face a problem that is outside any of its areas of expertise, an inevitable occurrence in an ever-changing world.

Perhaps the capacity to learn is enough to plug the gap here. In an unfamiliar situation, a new specialist skill can be learned. Well, the ability to learn is certainly needed to build up and maintain a repertoire of skills. Indeed, learning, in its various forms, is the backdrop to all intelligence. But learning is time-consuming and risky. The hallmark of properly general intelligence is the ability to adapt an existing behavioral repertoire to new challenges, and to do so without recourse to trial and error or to training by a third party.

1.2 Common Sense and Creativity

So what would it take to overcome the limitations of specialization, to endow a machine with properly general intelligence? Perhaps the foremost requirements for such a machine are *common sense* and *creativity*. To have common sense, in this context, is to display an understanding of the principles of operation of the everyday world, in particular the physical and social environments. For example, one such principle is that if you walk all the way around something, you end up back where you started. Another is that if you walk back along a path you have just followed, you encounter the same landmarks but in reverse order. Principles such as these are useful because their application is not confined to narrow domains. They are universal and reusable.

What does mastery of a principle of common sense entail? There is no need to say anything about mechanism to answer this question. In particular, there's no reason to assume that mastery necessitates the internal representation of the principle in some language-like form. Instead, it will be manifest in behavior. Or more likely, the lack of some aspect of common sense will be manifest in behavior.

For example, the cockerel that lives behind our house likes to fly up and over the gate, escaping his enclosure. But he's never out for long before he wants to get back in to rejoin the hens. All he needs to do is fly back over the gate. Yet this never occurs to him. Instead, he paces anxiously up and down in front of the gate. He seems to lack the commonsense principle that certain actions are reversible.

To the extent that such blind spots in understanding do not show up in an animal's behavior, it might be said to possess common sense. Of course, these considerations apply to humans as well as other animals, where they extend into the social realm. In particular, a shared understanding of the everyday world is at the core of language. Suppose you turn up to work to find a group of colleagues standing outside the building in the rain. "What are you doing?" you ask the nearest person. You would find it odd if she replied, albeit truthfully, "I'm standing in the rain." Instead she says "Fire alarm," and thereby exhibits a commonsense understanding of the human need for information and the role of conversation in obtaining it.

The second major requirement for general intelligence is creativity. The sort of creativity in question is not that of a great artist or composer or mathematician, but something every human being is capable of, something displayed by children in abundance. It is the ability to innovate, to generate novel behavior, to invent new things or devise new ways to use old things. It might be exploratory, or playful, as when a child improvises a dance. But it might be more goal-directed, such as planning the layout of a garden or devising ways to reduce household spending. Little creative acts such as these may not seem novel in the grand scheme of human affairs, but in each case they require the individual to go beyond his or her established behavioral repertoire, to reshape its elements or to assemble them in previously untried combinations.

Creativity and common sense complement each other. Creativity enables the individual to come up with new actions, but a commonsense understanding of the everyday world is needed to anticipate the consequences of those actions. On one hand, creativity without common sense (as we're using the terms here) is nothing more than thrashing in the dark. On the other hand, common sense without creativity is inflexible. But an intelligence that can wield both is a powerful thing. Confronted with an unfamiliar challenge, it can entertain a multitude of possibilities for action thanks to its creative faculty and, thanks to its commonsense understanding of their effects, anticipate each of their likely outcomes before twitching a muscle or spinning a motor.

A fine example of apparently spontaneous innovation was reported in 2002 by a team of scientists from Oxford led by animal cognition researcher Alex Kacelnik.[4] They were studying tool use in captive New Caledonian crows (an especially clever species), using an experimental apparatus comprising a small bucket containing food and a tall tube. To challenge the birds, the bucket was lowered into the tube, so that the handle was just out of reach. The birds were provided with pieces of bent wire, which they soon learned to use as hooks to lift the food-bucket out. However, on one occasion, when no hooks were available to the birds, only a piece of straight wire was left in their enclosure. Without ever having been trained to do so, one of the birds, Betty, jammed one end of the wire into a hole in the apparatus and bent it into a hook, which she then used to retrieve the food.

Betty's action was a blend of creativity and common sense. It required creativity to come up with the very idea of bending an otherwise useless piece of wire, and it required a common sense understanding of the pliable materials to anticipate the outcome. If these cognitive ingredients can produce impressive results in nonhuman animals, how much greater are their benefits in language-using humans. The schoolboy who hurls an inventive insult at one of his classmates blends linguistic creativity with a commonsense understanding of human psychology (even if he lacks the common sense not to aim such an insult at the teacher). This is a trivial example. But every human achievement, from the pyramids to the moon landings, is the product of a myriad such acts of invention, layered one upon another. A human-level artificial general intelligence must display a similar blend of common sense and creativity if it is to perform comparable feats.

1.3 The Space of Possible AIs

If the requirements for artificial general intelligence are so clear—all it needs is a little creativity and a little common sense—then why was so little progress made in the first sixty years of research in the field? Given the lack of success, is there any reason to suppose that human-level AI is practicable? And given that human-level AI is so difficult to create, what is the point of speculating about superintelligent AI? We have been examining the *behavioral* hallmarks of general intelligence, and have so far avoided discussion of the *mechanisms* by which it might be realized, either in the biological brain or in an artifact. But before we can address these questions, this omission needs to be remedied. We cannot begin to paint a picture of the future of AI without thinking about concrete mechanisms. In computer science terms, we need to think not just about specification but also about implementation.

It is a commonplace in computer science that the same specification can be implemented in many ways. This makes our task a difficult one because, unlike a software company that only needs to produce a single product, we would like to form an idea of the *whole space* of possible artificial intelligences. Moreover, for all we know, some revolutionary technology will be developed in the near future that will enable the creation of artificial general intelligence of a kind that we can barely imagine today.

We cannot begin to paint a picture of the future of AI without thinking about concrete mechanisms. In computer science terms, we need to think not just about specification but also about implementation.

Nevertheless, we have little choice but to start with the variety of schools in current AI research, and attempt to extrapolate from there.

One axis along which the space of possible AIs can usefully be classified is biological fidelity. How closely does the operation of an AI mimic that of the biological brain? At one end of this axis we find AIs that have been engineered from scratch, according to principles quite different from those that govern biological intelligence. At the other end of the axis are machines based on neural networks that copy biological brains down to a fine level of physical detail. There have been methodological schools advocating work at all points along this spectrum throughout the history of AI. The popularity of each school has waxed and waned, but none has emerged as triumphant, and each has arguments in its favor.

For example, a well-worn analogy with the history of powered flight likens the first type of machine, the AI engineered from scratch, to an aeroplane. Early designs for flying machines included flapping wings, imitating birds. But this approach failed. Fixed wings and propellers turned out to be the best way to get a large, heavy, human-made object airborne. Similarly, according to the argument by analogy, artificial intelligence shouldn't proceed by trying to imitate nature, but by devising a whole new set of engineering principles tailored for silicon-based computation.

As well as being a viable step toward the future creation of artificial general intelligence, whole brain emulation is touted as the route to *mind uploading*, an important goal for certain brands of transhumanism.

Opponents of this standpoint (after pointing out the dubious status of arguments by analogy) can counter that the biological brain is the only exemplar we have of general intelligence. We know it's possible to implement general intelligence in a neural substrate. Insofar as we can replicate this substrate artificially, we can be confident of success. Indeed, in its most extreme, brute-force guise, this biologically inspired approach is almost guaranteed to succeed under certain fairly conservative scientific and technological assumptions.

There's a lot to say about engineering AI from scratch, and we'll return to this theme in due course. But it is this brute-force biologically inspired approach, known as *whole brain emulation*, that will be our focus for the time being.[5] As well as being a viable step toward the future creation of artificial general intelligence, whole brain emulation is touted as the route to *mind uploading*, an important goal for certain brands of transhumanism. Finally, the mere concept of whole brain emulation is useful as a philosophical thought experiment. It forms the basis of a cluster of potent philosophical arguments relating to the very idea of artificial intelligence, to *machine consciousness*, and to personal identity, all of which are highly relevant to the topic of this book.

WHOLE BRAIN EMULATION

2.1 Copying the Brain

What exactly is whole brain emulation? In a nutshell, the idea is to make an exact working copy (or copies) of a particular brain in a nonbiological (e.g., computational) substrate. To understand the details, we need to know a bit of basic neuroscience. The vertebrate brain, like every other organ in an animal's body, comprises a multitude of cells. Many of these cells are *neurons*, which are remarkable electrical devices, each one capable of sophisticated signal processing. A neuron consists of a cell body (called the soma), an *axon*, and a set of *dendrites*. Crudely speaking, the dendrites can be thought of as the neuron's input and the axon as its output, while the soma does the signal processing.

Neurons are richly interconnected, and they form a complex network. Both axons and dendrites resemble trees, with numerous branches fanning out and inter-twining with the axons and dendrites of other neurons. At points where the axon (output) of one neuron is very close to a dendrite (input) of another neuron, a *synapse* can form. By means of a complex exchange of chemicals, a synapse permits signals to jump from one neuron to an-other, which allows them to communicate with each other. The human brain contains an astonishing number of neu-rons—more than 80 billion. But neurons are not confined to an animal's *central* nervous system, its brain and spinal cord. The *peripheral* nervous system is also constituted by neurons, which carry sensory signals to the brain from the body—the skin, the eyes, the stomach, and so on—and carry motor signals from the brain (via the spinal cord) to the rest of the body, to the muscles, the glands, and so on.

Activity in the brain results from the interplay of elec-trical and chemical activity. In particular, the behavior of a neuron is modulated by the presence of chemical *neu-rotransmitters*, such as dopamine and seratonin. These chemicals are produced by special-purpose neurons with long, diffuse axonal projections that disseminate the chemicals throughout the brain. Neuromodulating chemi-cals can also be delivered to the brain via the blood, which is how most psychoactive drugs work.

The brain isn't just made of neurons. It also contains a vascular system that transports blood to all its parts, de-livering the energy it needs to generate all those electrical signals. And it contains a vast number of so-called glial cells. These were once thought of simply as a kind of glue, holding all the neurons and their axons and dendrites in place. But the glial cells seem to perform a signaling function of their own, albeit on a slower timescale than the neurons.

The signaling properties of individual neurons are more-or-less understood. The details are complicated. But simply put, each neuron adds up (integrates) the signals on its dendritic input, and when the total reaches a threshold, it emits a pulse, or *spike*, along its axon. Precise descriptions of this process have been around since the 1950s, when Alan Hodgkin and Andrew Huxley formalized the mathematical model for which they earned the Nobel Prize in medicine.

An essential property of the brain is its *plasticity*. During development, the connections in the pre-natal and infantile brain undergo dramatic reconfiguration, as axons and dendrites grow like the roots of a plant, feeling their way across enormous distances (in neural terms) to establish new connections, as well as abandoning redundant ones. Additionally, throughout an animal's life, established neural connections are subject to constant changes in strength, facilitating learning and memory. Good mathematical models exist of these plastic processes too.

Obviously this brief overview doesn't even scratch the surface of what we know about the brain, and what we do know barely scratches the surface of all there is to know. However, everything in our burgeoning understanding of its inner workings lends supports the following hypothesis, which is enormously significant both practically and philosophically: human behavior is determined by physical processes in the brain that mediate between its incoming sensory signals and its outgoing motor signals.

Of course, to make sense of human behavior we have to see it in the context of an embodied animal interacting with its physical and social environment. Activity in the brain is meaningless otherwise. But this platitude is irrelevant to the hypothesis. Put another way, the claim is simply that there are no causal mysteries, no missing links, in the (immensely complicated) chain of causes and effects that leads from what we see, hear, and touch to what we do and say. The possibility of whole brain emulation rests on this claim.

2.2 Three Stages of Whole Brain Emulation

The business of whole brain emulation can be envisioned as a three-stage process: mapping, simulation, and embodiment.[1] The first stage is to map the brain of the subject at high (submicron) spatial resolution. The entire forebrain (at least) should be included in the map. This ensures that the portions of the brain most closely associated with higher cognitive functions are scanned, notably the cerebral cortex (gray matter) and its interconnections (white matter), as well as structures associated with emotion and action selection, such as the amygdala and the basal ganglia. The mapping process should acquire (at least) the location and characteristics of every neuron and every synapse, along with a neuron-level *connectome*, that is to say a record of every connection between every axon and every dendrite. The result will be an exquisitely detailed blueprint of a particular brain at a particular time.

The second stage of the process is to use this blueprint to build a real-time simulation of the electrochemical activity of all of those neurons and their connections. Such a simulation could, for example, be built using standard techniques from the field of computational neuroscience, using established mathematical formulations of neuronal behavior such as the Hodgkin–Huxley model. The underlying techniques here are much the same as those used to simulate the weather, say, or fluid flow around a wing. It goes without saying that considerable computing resources would be needed to simulate even a small brain this way.

The third stage of the process is to interface the simulation to an external environment. So far all we have is a very complicated, disembodied computing device. To bridge the gap from a powerless *simulation* running inside a box to a causally potent *emulation* that exhibits outward behavior necessitates the construction of a body (even if this is a

The business of whole brain emulation can be envisioned as a three-stage process: mapping, simulation, and embodiment.

simulated body in a virtual world—a possibility I discuss later). Since the simulation expects incoming signals just like those of its biological precursor, and generates outgoing signals just like those of its biological precursor, the task of interfacing the simulated brain to this (synthetic) body is made easier if it is morphologically and mechanically similar to the body of the original animal.

If the mapping and simulation stages are successful, then the behavior of the simulated neurons, both individually and as a population, should be effectively indistinguishable from that of the original, biological brain given the same input from the environment. The word "effectively" is important here because it would be too much to expect a perfect match. A brain is a chaotic system, in the mathematical sense that very small differences in initial conditions can lead to very large differences in the behavior of the system over time. Consequently small inaccuracies in the mapping process, as well as numerical rounding errors in the computation, would cause the behavior of the simulation eventually to diverge from that of its biological prototype.

But this limitation isn't necessarily a barrier to successful emulation. If these microscopic deviations are sufficiently small, the macro-scale outward behavior of the emulation would surely be indistinguishable from that of the original. From the standpoint of an observer, the emulation would seem to make the same decisions and to perform the same actions as its prototype under any given set of circumstances. If the subject is human, then even his or her friends and loved ones would have to admit that the emulation behaved uncannily like the person they knew, displaying the same habits, talking in the same way, even claiming to possess the same memories.

2.3   The Technology of Brain Mapping

The idea of human whole brain emulation is technologically problematic and philosophically challenging. It's a theme we will return to in due course. But for now, let's consider a species that raises fewer technological and philosophical difficulties, one with a smaller brain, namely the mouse. What would it take to achieve whole brain emulation for a mouse? What kind of technology would be required? Let's take each of the three stages of emulation in turn.

Here is one way to carry out a detailed structural scan of a mouse's brain using early 21st century technology. First, the (un)fortunate mouse is killed and its brain extracted. Second, its forebrain is sectioned into ultra-thin slices. Third, each slice is imaged and digitized using electron microscopy. Fourth, the placement and type of each neuron, the shape of each axon and dendrite, the location and type of each synapse, and so on, are all reconstructed by computer from the stack of images. The result would be a very large dataset capturing much of the essence of the original brain, just the sort of blueprint we need.

But would it be sufficient to construct an emulation? A structural scan of this sort only provides a snapshot of the brain's components frozen in time—what their shapes are, how they are arranged, how they connect one to another. It doesn't directly tell us about dynamics, about how those components behave and interact. The higher the spatial resolution of the structural scan, the smaller the neural microstructures it will include, and the easier it will be to reconstruct the likely behavior of a given neuron on a computer using a mathematical model. Nevertheless, even a high-resolution scan is unlikely to be able to fix all the parameters required by such a model, such as the strength of a synaptic connection. And without all its parameters filled in, a mathematical model is useless for computer simulation.

However, if they can be obtained, recordings of the electrical activity of a neuron can compensate for shortcomings even in a lower resolution structural scan. One possible method for doing this, again using early 21st century technology, is to use a mouse that has been genetically modified so that its neurons produce a dye that fluoresces when they fire. Then, by shining light onto the cortex, recordings can be made of the activity of every neuron in the brain using ordinary light microscopy.[2] (Obviously these have to be made before the mouse is killed and its brain sliced.) Automated techniques can subsequently be used to search for values for the missing parameters such that, when plugged into the model, the recorded data are most accurately reproduced.

Scanning and recording techniques such as these are very promising. However, the brain of a mouse contains over 70 million neurons, and each neuron can have several thousand synaptic connections. A human brain contains over 80 billion neurons and tens of trillions of synapses. Computationally intensive methods such as the slice-and-scan procedure will struggle with the sheer numbers involved, and even Moore's law is unlikely to bail these methods out. The fluorescence microscopy method described also has its limitations. Although it has excellent spatial resolution, and can monitor individual neurons, it has relatively low temporal resolution and cannot distinguish individual spiking events. Thankfully, though, various alternative approaches to mapping the brain are on the horizon, due to advances in biotechnology and nanotechnology. Let's take a look at a couple of candidates.

We just touched on one relevant application of genetic engineering. Here is another.[3] Suppose that we can genetically engineer the mouse so that every neuron in its brain contains a sequence embedded in its DNA that is unique to that neuron, a kind of "DNA barcode." Then, with every neuron individually barcoded, the mouse's brain could be "infected" with an otherwise harmless virus that has been specially engineered to carry genetic material across synaptic gaps, enabling DNA from the pre-synaptic neuron to recombine with DNA from the post-synaptic neuron. This would produce new strands of DNA, each containing a pair of barcodes representing the existence of a synaptic connection between the two neurons in question.

The brain of the mouse would thus become a repository of billions of genetically encoded records of pairwise connections between neurons. The task then would be to extract these data, which could be done using DNA sequencing technology. With this method, a neuron-level connectome would be obtainable without the costly intermediate step, in terms of data and computation, of submicron-scale imaging and image processing. Moreover the bottleneck with this method, the speed and cost of DNA sequencing, has undergone years of exponential improvement in the aftermath of the human genome project.

So this is a promising technique. But as with the slice-and-scan procedure described earlier, it would only supply some of the data necessary to emulate the brain. It reveals structure but not function. This is where nanotechnology comes in. Nanotechnology could help map the mouse's neural activity, and thereby it could fill in the missing details of the blueprint. Biotechnology and nanotechnology both rely on the same powerful idea—the exploitation of very large numbers of very small objects. In the case of biotechnology, the very small objects in question are biological—viruses, bacteria, strands of DNA, and so on. But the idea works just as well with very small nonbiological objects. The field of nanotechnology concerns the manufacture of such objects, objects whose characteristic size is of the order of tens of nanometers, that is to say a few tens of billionths of a meter.

Nanotechnology has numerous potential applications, many of which are relevant to this book. But for now we'll confine our attention to the business of brain activity mapping. At the nano-scale, even the soma of a neuron, whose characteristic size is a few millionths of a meter, looks big. So we can imagine creating swarms of nano-scale robots capable of swimming freely in the brain's network of blood vessels, each one then attaching itself like a limpet to the membrane of a neuron or close to a synapse.[4] There it would sit, sensing the neuron's fluctuating membrane potential or detecting spike events, and transmitting this information live to a fleet of micro-scale way-station devices near the cortical surface. The job of these way stations would be to harvest incoming data from the numerous "neuro-limpets" and to broadcast to the outside world, where the data can be collected by the neuroscientist.

Although these are speculative proposals, they hint at what may be feasible in the near future. It's not the aim of this book to make detailed predictions or to guess at the timescale of technological progress. Rather, the aim is to work through a range of possible future scenarios and their ramifications. The specific point here is that the barriers to providing a blueprint for the mouse brain, a blueprint with sufficient detail to enable a successful emulation, are technological not conceptual. Moreover they are barriers that are likely to be overcome in due course, perhaps using some combination of biotechnology and nanotechnology. It may take ten years. Perhaps it will take fifty. But historically speaking, even a century would be a very short time.

In the meantime there is another possibility to consider, one that would require less scaling up in scanning technology but more science. So far we have been thinking about attempting to copy the brain of a particular adult animal. If the copy is to be behaviorally indistinguishable from the original, faithfully reproducing all its learned behavior, all its habits and preferences, a very detailed, very accurate scan would be required. But suppose instead that a large number of brains of newborn mice were scanned in as much detail as the state-of-the-art technology allowed. Then, by merging all the data, and drawing on as much other mouse brain data as possible to constrain it, a statistical model of the *average neonate* mouse brain could be built.[5]

With the aid of such a statistical model, any number of precise, neuron-by-neuron, synapse-by-synapse descriptions of individual juvenile mouse brains could be *generated*, each differing a little from the other but each conforming to the overall statistical template. None of these descriptions would correspond to the brain of a real mouse that had actually lived. But, given enough data to sufficiently constrain the model, each would represent a viable mouse brain, ready to be instantiated in a computer simulation and embodied.

2.4 The Technology of Neural Simulation

With a detailed description of the brain duly acquired by some means or another, the simulation can be put together. There are a variety of options for the underlying substrate on which the simulation might be implemented. These range from conventional digital computers through custom-made analogue hardware to chemical or biological computers. The most conventional route to implementation involves the kind of digital computer we all have on our desks or embedded in our mobile phones. Any conventional digital computer can be used to simulate, one small time step at a time, how a collection of variables changes given a set of differential equations governing those variables. The electrical and chemical properties of the various components of a neuron can be modeled this way, for example, using the Hodgkin–Huxley equations mentioned previously.

Of course, the task at hand is to simulate not just a single neuron but many neurons connected together. So there are many variables, each governed by the equations in question, and the task is to simulate them all at once.

How can this be done in real time on a conventional, serial computer, which in effect carries out only one operation at a time? Well, fortunately neurons are slow. Even when excited, a typical neuron only emits a spike every few milliseconds. In the time it takes for a typical neuron to emit two spikes, a desktop computer running at a modest 3 GHz can perform more than ten million operations. So it's possible to simulate many neurons at once by multi-tasking. In each millisecond of simulated time, the computer spends a tiny fraction of a millisecond simulating neuron 1, a tiny fraction of a millisecond simulating neuron 2, and so on for tens of thousands of neurons.

However, even the brain of a mouse contains tens of millions of neurons, and to simulate them all accurately and in real time requires an awful lot of computation. Although processor clock speeds increased at a gratifyingly exponential rate in the 1980s and 1990s, this trend eventually slowed in the early 21st century. Even the fastest serial processor cannot simulate all the neurons in a mouse's brain. Fortunately, though, *parallelism* can take the strain at this point. Rather than using a serial processor that carries out one operation at a time, the simulation can be done with multiple processors all running simultaneously, each one simulating many thousands of neurons. Just as it's possible for a thousand workers to build, in a week, a brick edifice that would take an individual bricklayer a lifetime, it's possible to simulate a whole brain using numerous slow parallel processors, something that would be impossible to simulate in real time using one fast processor.

Indeed the brain itself exploits a form of massive parallelism. Each neuron might be thought of as a tiny, independent information-processing unit. Its input is the set of signals on its dendrites. It has a memory in the form of various physical quantities, such as its membrane potential and the strengths of its synapses. And the neuron itself "computes" a function that continuously maps its dendritic "input" and the current state of its "memory" to the "output" signal it delivers to its axon. The underlying functional substrate of the brain, according to this analogy, is a form of massively parallel computation, with many millions of tiny processors all working simultaneously.

The analogy with parallel computation breaks down somewhat when we look at the real physics and chemistry of a neuron.[6] But it helps to illustrate an important point, which is that the biological brain is another example of the principle of exploiting very large numbers of very small things. In order to simulate the brain, we need to exercise the same principle, albeit in a different substrate. So it bodes well for the prospect of whole brain emulation that the supercomputers of the mid-2010s are all massively parallel machines. Moreover, as the number of processors they incorporate has increased, the cost per processor has gone down, following an exponential trend that accords with Moore's law.

This particular technological trend owes a good deal to legions of computer gamers, whose demand for a better gaming experience has driven the development of cheap, high-performance graphics processing units (GPUs). Although originally dedicated to manipulating large arrays of pixels, the architecture of a GPU is essentially that of a general-purpose parallel computer. As their efficiency and power increased and their cost went down, they found new applications in other areas requiring large numbers of parallel calculations, such as modeling nuclear reactions or the climate. By 2012 the world's most powerful computer, Cray's Titan, was based on a hybrid architecture that incorporated 18,688 GPUs, each one in itself a powerful parallel computer.

2.5 Brain-Scale Computation

It would already be possible to simulate the whole brain of a mouse using the most powerful computers of the mid-2010s if (1) the level of physical detail required for successful emulation were sufficiently low and (2) we had a blueprint at the required level of detail. We have already discussed some of the technological options for meeting the second condition. As for the first condition, the jury is still out. Is it possible to achieve behavioral indistinguishability while abstracting away from the chemistry of synaptic transmission, the structure of glial cells, the shapes of dendrites and axons, and so on, and treating neurons as simple, point-like, mathematical objects? If so, then the computational demands of whole brain emulation would be orders of magnitude less than if all these aspects of the brain had to be modeled.

Neuroscience has yet to answer this question. But even if the answer is favorable, the scale-up from a mouse brain to a human brain (and to human-level intelligence) is huge. The engineering challenge here is not merely to achieve the required number of FLOPS (floating point operations per second) but to do so in a small volume and with low power consumption. The average human brain (male) occupies a mere 1,250 cm^3 and consumes just 20 W. By contrast, the Tianhe-2, the world's most powerful supercomputer in 2013, consumes 24 MW and is housed in a complex occupying 720 m^2. Yet it still has only a fraction of the computing power needed to simulate a human brain under even the most conservative assumptions. In short, massive parallelism notwithstanding, it may be necessary to look beyond conventional digital computers to achieve human-level AI via the whole brain emulation route.

One promising approach is *neuromorphic* hardware.[7] Rather than using existing general-purpose computing technology, the idea here is to construct custom hardware that closely resembles the wetware of the brain. Conventional digital hardware performs hundreds of binary floating point arithmetic operations to simulate a few milliseconds of change in a single neuron's membrane potential. This involves thousands of transistor switching events, each of which consumes power (and generates heat). The membrane potential itself is represented as a binary number, which changes in discrete steps rather than varying continuously like a real physical quantity. The neuromorphic approach does away with all this digital paraphernalia and uses *analogue* components that behave like the original neuron. The membrane potential is represented by a real physical quantity of charge that undergoes continuous variation. The result is far more efficient in terms of power consumption.

When we looked at potential brain mapping technologies for whole brain emulation, we envisaged scaling up contemporary technology (e.g., slicing and scanning), or successfully developing nascent technologies that already look feasible (e.g., DNA barcoding), or effecting a paradigm shift to a theoretically possible but highly speculative technology (e.g., neural nanobots). With the technology of neural simulation, we can look at a similar range of possibilities. We have already discussed massively parallel supercomputers that use conventional, digital architectures, and we just touched on neuromorphic hardware, which is well established as an alternative technique for simulating small numbers of neurons but needs to be scaled up dramatically.

But what lies on the more distant horizon? There has been a good deal of speculation about the potential of quantum computation. This is certainly an interesting topic. But the class of problems for which quantum computation is theoretically advantageous does not include large-scale neural simulation. Exotic quantum effects, such as superposition, can be exploited to solve intractable search problems. But the computational demands of whole brain simulation are unrelated to the intractability of search.[8] They are dictated by the requirement for truly massive parallelism. What we really need is a hardware paradigm that would allow Moore's law to continue beyond the limits imposed by physics on the scale of integration possible in conventional hardware, limits such as the speed of light, the size of an atom, and the minimal energy required to flip a bit from one state to another.

One candidate is *quantum dot cellular automata* (QDCA).[9] Despite the use of the word "quantum" here, a QDCA is not a quantum computer. Rather, a quantum dot is a nano-scale semiconductor device that can act like a transistor, switching states very rapidly but using very little power. Four quantum dots can be arranged in a square to form a quantum dot cell, which can store a single bit of information. Quantum dot cells can be laid out on a grid (to form a cellular automaton) and organized into logic gates and communication channels. These are the basic elements of digital electronics, and they can be assembled into tiny processors.

The advantage of QDCA over conventional (complementary metal-oxide semiconductor or CMOS) silicon technology is the enormous scale of integration they permit, enabling many more switching devices to be placed in the same area than is physically possible with CMOS while consuming modest power and generating little heat. But the practical application of QDCA is perhaps decades away. In the nearer term the semiconductor industry is likely to retain conventional processor design, perhaps exploiting 3D stacks of transistors in an effort to prolong Moore's law as opposed to the 2D slices of silicon used today, and perhaps abandoning silicon altogether by adopting *carbon nanotubes* as the medium for constructing smaller, more efficient transistors.

One thing is beyond doubt. The electronics industry of the 2010s is a long way from producing computers that come anywhere near the ultimate theoretical limit to how much computation can be carried out within a given portion of matter. The term *computronium* is sometimes used to denote a (mythical) material within which the number of computational operations carried out per second is equal to the maximum physically possible in any configuration of atoms. The physicist Seth Lloyd has calculated that such a theoretically perfect computer with a mass of 1 kg and occupying a volume of 1 liter would perform 5.4×10^{50} logical operations per second on 10^{31} bits. This is a staggering 39 orders of magnitude greater than today's computers.[10]

There is little prospect of ever achieving this kind of computational power in practice. However, a tiny fraction of this capacity would be sufficient for a very high fidelity simulation of the human brain. After all, the human brain is only a little over a liter in volume and (astonishingly) consumes just 20 W of power. Whether we are talking about simulating large numbers of neurons or achieving AI via a less biologically inspired route, the real possibility of much more powerful computers than we have today is a major motivation for thinking through the possibility of machine superintelligence.

2.6   Robotics: The Technology of Embodiment

Let us suppose that, by some means or another, the technological obstacles to mapping and simulation have been overcome. An exquisitely detailed operational replica of the forebrain of a pioneer mouse has been constructed. The final stage of the emulation process is to interface the simulated brain to a synthetic (robot) body. Only at this stage can we properly test and tune the simulation to obtain the desired behavioral equivalence with the original. The robot body could in principle take a number of forms, more or less like the body of a mouse. But the interfacing problems are fewer if the body is as mouse-like as possible. So this is what we'll assume for now—not a hard-shelled body on wheels but a soft, four-legged body with a musculoskeletal system. Similarly let's imagine the robot body with a biomimetic suite of sensors—eyes, ears, and (very importantly) whiskers, all of which deliver a set of signals typical for these modalities in a real mouse.

Now we have, in one hand as it were, the simulated forebrain of the mouse, and in the other hand the synthetic mouse body. But how do we join them? We cannot simply plug one into the other. The problem is that, in the real animal, there is no neat separation between the forebrain and the rest of the body. In fact the forebrain is just a particularly dense concentration of neurons and connections at one end of a nervous system that permeates an animal's body from tip to toe, much as a system of rivers and tributaries permeates a rainforest. But we have elected to "sever" the forebrain from the rest of this system. In doing so, we threw away a large chunk of the central nervous system, including the cerebellum, which is implicated in motor coordination, and the whole of the peripheral nervous system.

There are good reasons to believe that the forebrain harbors much of the "essence" of a particular mouse, much as there is reason to believe that the forebrain of a human being harbors much of the what it means to be that particular human being—habits, preferences, expertise, memories, personality. So the decision to focus on the forebrain was justified. However, by choosing to map and simulate just the forebrain, it is as if we had torn a tapestry in half, and now we have to join it back together again, re-attaching one silken thread at a time so as to seamlessly restore the original pattern. Or worse, it's as if we had discarded one-half of the tapestry altogether and are now forced to synthesize the missing portion from scratch, guessing at the lost half of the pattern.

The mouse's body is the missing half of the tapestry, and the forebrain simulation, its myriad inputs and outputs disconnected like threads of torn silk dangling in the air, is the half of the tapestry we now have. Unfortunately, the inputs to and outputs from the forebrain simulation don't come with labels attached, stating which wires to connect them to in the robot body. The engineer somehow has to work out what patterns of muscular movement were originally caused by each of the brain's outgoing motor signals, and what incoming signals would originally have arisen from any given pattern of sensory stimulation. The precise location in cortex of a sensory neuron is a clue, especially in the case of vision and touch, whose connections are "topographically" organized. But this information falls a long way short of a wiring diagram that would make the job of the roboticist easy.

The root of the difficulty is that, in the animal prototype, the various parts of the whole system—the forebrain, the rest of the nervous system, and the rest of the body—grew and developed together, each adapting to each other's idiosyncrasies in an organic fashion. So one way to avoid the problem might be to widen the remit of the mapping stage. Instead of mapping just the forebrain, why not construct a map of the entire nervous system, central and peripheral, in tandem with a high-resolution representation of the 3D structure of the body? Then, as well as constructing a computer-simulated replica of the (entire) brain, we could synthesize an exact copy of the body of our particular mouse, including all the specifics of its very own peripheral nervous system and musculoskeletal structure. We are already in the business of extrapolating relevant technologies, so why should we not expect our capabilities in this sphere to extend to the body as a whole?

Alternatively, rather than acquiring a scan of the whole peripheral nervous system and musculoskeletal structure, machine learning techniques could be applied, while the subject of the emulation is alive, to figure out the relationship between the brain's sensorimotor activity and the movements that result. Knowing this relationship, an interface could be constructed that translates motor signals generated by the brain into commands that the robot's synthetic body can understand (and supplies the brain with the proprioceptive signals and haptic feedback it expects). A plus point for this approach is that it reduces the extent to which the synthetic body has to resemble the original. If the emulation is to work out of the box, with a bare minimum of tuning and calibration, then the basic body pattern would have to be preserved—complete with four legs, paws, and twitchable nose in the case of the mouse. But thanks to clever interfacing, there would be no need to reproduce the mouse's exact set of muscles and their characteristics.

The need for a close replica of the original body is also reduced if we exploit another powerful learning device which is at our disposal, namely the simulated brain itself. The biological brain is a master of adaptation. Humans can learn to drive cars, to fly planes, to operate cranes and diggers, and so on. For the skilled driver, pilot, or operator, a machine can become an extension of the body. Moreover people who suffer horrific, disabling injuries have an extraordinary capacity to adjust to their predicament, learning to use wheelchairs, artificial limbs, and other prosthetics. A simulated brain would be no less plastic, no less adaptive. As long as the emulation is not expected to work right out of the box, there is no need for a body that works with sensorimotor signals perfectly matching those of the original. A period of training, or "rehabilitation," can compensate for the mismatch.

Using a combination of these two methods—engineering an interface tailored to behavioral data *and* introducing a period of rehabilitation—the range of body patterns available to the emulation could be greatly expanded. Why confine the emulated mouse to a mouse's body? The reanimated creature could have six legs, or wheels. If the engineers have a mathematical model of the neural pattern

The biological brain is a
master of adaptation.

corresponding to, say, the urge to "move toward the object in the center of the visual field," then they can ensure that the mouse's synthetic body moves toward the object in the mouse's visual field whenever the mouse's synthetic brain wants it to.

Not only could the simulated brain adapt to an unfamiliar body, the new body could also be designed to adapt to the simulated brain thanks to advances in the fields of prosthetics and brain-machine interfaces. Contemporary human prosthetics are not passive devices. Rather, they are capable of shaping complex movements independently (as indeed are the tentacles of an octopus). But to do this effectively, they have to learn to recognize the intentions of their hosts. The field of brain-machine interfaces is making rapid progress in the application of machine learning to this problem, and the techniques it develops can also help with whole brain emulation. If the simulated brain and the synthetic body were allowed to co-adapt, then rehabilitation with a novel body pattern would be greatly facilitated.

2.7   Virtual Embodiment

The biological brain is part of a sensorimotor loop, which enables it to direct the movements, in continuous time, of a body situated in a world with three spatial dimensions. A functional simulation of an animal's brain must also be part of sensorimotor loop, and its inputs and outputs must be functionally equivalent to those of a real brain, which necessitates its embodiment. Interfacing the simulated brain to a *physical*, robotic body is one way to achieve this. Another way is to build a detailed *simulation* of the animal's body and of the physical environment it normally lives in. The simulated mouse brain can be interfaced to a simulated mouse body (complete with simulated paws, whiskers, and fur), and let loose in a virtual world containing simulated grass, simulated hedges, and simulated cheese, all rendered with high enough resolution to be effectively indistinguishable from the real thing as far as the mouse's sensorimotor apparatus is concerned.

The techniques for doing this are well established, and once again we have to thank the economic clout of the video gamer for this. Thanks to the demand for an ever more photorealistic gaming experience, developers have produced ever more sophisticated *physics engines* that can simulate the behavior of physical objects in virtual worlds. The physics engine maintains the positions and orientations of the numerous objects that exist in the world of the game as they move around and bump into each other, taking account of the effects of gravity, friction, and so on. The reason for maintaining this information in a computer game is to render objects from the viewpoint of the gamer's character (or perhaps from a viewpoint just behind the character). In the context of virtual embodiment, the role of the physics engine would be to provide realistic input and output for the simulated brain.

But the engineering challenge is the same, whether the application is gaming or virtual embodiment. Solid objects are relatively straightforward to simulate. Soft or flexible objects, such as muscles or blades of grass, present more difficulties. Particulate matter, such as smoke or dust, is even trickier. But graphics experts have long cracked all these cases. Other agents, which would be a requirement for any simulated brain belonging to a social animal, present special difficulties. They might be crudely simulated, like the so-called AIs in contemporary games, with a simple repertoire of stereotyped behaviors. But they might be the avatars of humans living in the real world. Or they might be other, fully realized AIs with general intelligence.

The last of these options raises the possibility of a whole virtual society of artificial intelligences living in a simulated environment. Liberated from the constraints of real biology and relieved of the need to compete for resources such as food and water, certain things become feasible for a virtual society that are not feasible for a society of agents who are confined to wetware. For example, given sufficient computing resources, a virtual society could operate at hyper-real speeds. Every millisecond that passed in the virtual world could be simulated in, say, one-tenth of a millisecond in the real world.

If a society of AIs inhabiting such a virtual world were to work on improving themselves or on creating even more intelligent successors, then from the standpoint of the real world their progress would be duly accelerated. And if they were able to direct their technological expertise back out to the real world and help improve the computational substrate on which they depended, then the rate of this acceleration would in turn be accelerated. This is one route to a singularity-like scenario. The result would be explosive technological change, and the consequences would be unpredictable.

2.8 Emulation and Enhancement

Let's get back to the more immediate future. Whole brain emulation is just one way to achieve artificial general intelligence, a point in the space of engineering possibilities at the far end of biological fidelity. However, it is a significant point in that space because it suggests that at least one brand of (mouse-level) artificial general intelligence will become feasible in the near term under fairly conservative philosophical, scientific, and technological assumptions.

Chief among these assumptions are that (1) intelligent behavior in humans and other animals is mediated by brain activity, which is governed by the laws of physics; (2) the level of physical detail necessary to achieve effective indistinguishability of behavior in an emulation is not too fine grained; and (3) existing mapping and computing technologies will scale sufficiently (by perhaps two or three orders of magnitude for a mouse) within a sufficiently short period. (A period short enough to get the attention of most people is "within their lifetime" or perhaps "within their children's lifetimes.")

The first assumption represents a philosophical position that most would accept. The second assumption begs a number of scientific questions. It entails, for example, that we can get away with not simulating individual glial cells, that the continuous (as opposed to discrete) nature of the biological brain is not an obstacle to simulation, and that we can disregard quantum effects altogether. The third assumption, as long as we stick with the mouse, is realistic as far as computing power is concerned and reasonable as far as brain mapping technology is concerned. So it's hard to avoid the conclusion that mouse-level artificial general intelligence is not only possible, but is a near term prospect.

Once a mouse-scale whole brain emulation has been achieved, there are compelling reasons to think that human-level AI would not be far off. There are a number of ways the transition could be made. The most obvious is simply to scale up the emulation process and apply it to the human brain. It would be hard engineering, for sure, but no conceptual breakthroughs would be required. But is it realistic to expect the relevant enabling technologies, such as computer processing power and storage capacity, to carry on improving at a fast enough rate? Moore's law has to end somewhere. Perhaps it will grind to a halt somewhere in the three orders of magnitude between mouse-scale whole brain emulation and human-scale whole brain emulation.

Yet we know it's *possible* to assemble billions of ultra-low power, nano-scale components into a device capable of human-level intelligence. Our own brains are the existence proof. Nature has done it, and we should be able to manipulate matter with the same facility as nature. So for sheer neuron count, we should eventually be able to match nature in the arena of brain-building, using some combination of synthetic biology and nanotechnology if we can do it no other way. Nevertheless, to meet the computational requirements of human-scale whole brain emulation might require a series of significant technological breakthroughs. In that case, scaling up the emulation process would not be an easy route to human-level AI.

However, human-scale whole brain emulation isn't the only option for upgrading to human-level AI. Perhaps the mouse-scale emulation itself could be cognitively enhanced. The most obvious (and perhaps naïve) way to attempt this would be simply to increase the neuron count in various cognitively important brain areas, such as the prefrontal cortex and the hippocampus. More plausibly, progress in understanding how cognition is realized in the vertebrate brain would be accelerated thanks to the availability of the mouse emulation as a research tool. This burgeoning theoretical knowledge could then be called on to help engineer suitable neural enhancements (or cognitive prostheses), while preserving the core mouse brain simulation.[11]

On this view, the mouse brain emulation is again the catalyst for achieving human-level AI. Like a particle accelerator in physics, a mouse-scale whole brain emulation would permit experiments to be carried out that could otherwise only be imagined. For example, it would be possible to observe the synthetic mouse's brain activity and behavior under carefully controlled conditions, and then to reset the whole system and re-run the same experiment with a small variation, such as a minute alteration to the brain. This is just the sort of experimental program that would allow the mouse's brain to be *reverse engineered*, and in due course we would no doubt learn enough to be able to design and build cognitive prostheses for it from first principles.

But would this be enough to get us to human-level AI, or would that require something more? For example, it would be vital to endow the enhanced mouse emulation with language. This would surely necessitate more than simply an increase in neuron count. It might require circuitry of a kind that is found nowhere in the brains of small vertebrates. Perhaps, in the human brain, evolution discovered some radical innovation, a qualitatively different type of neural mechanism, one capable of handling symbolic representation, combinatorial syntax, and compositional semantics, the building blocks of language.

If this is true, a complete theory of the mouse brain would still be insufficient, and the path from mouse-scale emulation to human-level AI would be less straightforward. But we shouldn't forget that, in parallel with the work of the neural engineers, neuroscientists will be unravelling the secrets of the human brain, without resorting to full-blown emulation but using increasingly powerful tools for mapping its structure and activity. Understanding the neural basis of language is, of course, a major target for neuroscience. So perhaps, by the time the engineers can put together a mouse-scale whole brain emulation, the neuroscientists will be in a position to help them devise a neural prosthesis that will confer language on a suitably enhanced mouse-scale emulation.

In short, a mouse-scale whole brain emulation would have the potential to kick-start progress toward human-level AI in a number of ways. Arguably, given human-level AI, the transition to superhuman-level AI would be almost inevitable. Human-level intelligence realized in a synthetic substrate would be more amenable to enhancement than the biological brain with its various limitations (low speed, reliance on metabolism, the need for sleep, etc.). Moreover the human-level AI itself (or indeed a team of human-level AIs) could be set to work on the problem, initiating a feedback loop of ever faster improvement and perhaps precipitating an *intelligence explosion* with unpredictable consequences. In other words, once we have achieved mouse-level artificial intelligence through whole brain emulation, the genie could be out of the bottle.

ENGINEERING AI

3.1 Intimations of Intelligence

We have devoted a lot of discussion so far to the brain-inspired route to human-level AI, and to whole brain emulation in particular. But the space of possible artificial intelligences is likely to be very diverse, and biological forms might occupy just a small corner of it. What does the rest of this space of possibilities look like? This is a very important question because the way an AI is built will shape its behavior, and will determine our ability to predict or control it.

It would be a serious mistake, perhaps a dangerous one, to imagine that the space of possible AIs is full of beings like ourselves, with goals and motives that resemble human goals and motives. Moreover, depending on how it was constructed, the way an AI or a collective of AIs set about achieving its aims (insofar as this notion even made sense) might be utterly inscrutable, like the workings of the alien intelligence Kasparov discerned across the chessboard. If the AI were the product of another AI, or if it were the outcome of self-modification or artificial evolution, then its potential inscrutability would be all the greater.

So which design and construction methods are more or less likely to lead to AI that is unpredictable and hard to control? The better we understand the space of possibilities, the better equipped we will be to address this question and mitigate the risk of building, and losing control of, the "wrong kind" of AI. Let's begin by looking at some examples of contemporary (mid-2010s) AI technology. Can we discern in these systems the beginnings of artificial general intelligence? Will general intelligence be achieved just by improving and extending such systems? Or is there something fundamental missing, a vital ingredient that must be added before AI technology truly takes off?

We'll start with an example of a disembodied AI application, namely the personal assistant. In the previous chapter the importance of embodiment was emphasized. But many of the fictional examples of artificial intelligence familiar to our culture are disembodied. Think of HAL, the errant computer in *2001: A Space Odyssey*. In a sense, the spacecraft in *2001* could be thought of as HAL's body. It has a well-defined spatial location, and it has sensors and actuators through which it interacts with its environment in continuous time. But at one point in the movie we are treated to scenes of HAL's early "life" in an Earth-bound laboratory, and the viewer is somehow persuaded that his intelligence is independent of the spacecraft. Our willingness to suspend disbelief here suggests that disembodied AI is conceptually possible. But is it possible in practice, and how far are we from achieving it?

Personal assistants such as Apple's Siri and Google Now showcase decades of gradual improvement in speech recognition. Without prior training on individual users, they are able to turn ordinary speech into text even in the presence of background noise and despite large variations in timbre and accent. Interestingly, the task of speech recognition often isn't carried out on the user's device. Raw sound files are streamed over the Internet to corporate processing centers, where the speech recognition is done and the corresponding text file is produced. So not only are these applications disembodied in the sense that they don't engage with an environment through sensorimotor interaction, even their processing and memory is dispersed in the cloud. Does this make them somehow "even more" disembodied? No. We can imagine a fully embodied, robotic system all of whose processing takes place off-board and in the cloud. But the point is worth noting.

In parallel with turning raw sound data into text, the personal assistant has to try to "understand" what the user is asking it to find out or instructing it to do. This is a considerable challenge in itself, even given a perfect transcription of a sound file into text. However, the task is made easier with the aid of a statistical model of the sorts of things people say, constructed from a huge database of examples. Given the beginning of a question or command, this enables the system to predict how it is most likely to continue. Moreover this prediction can be fed back to the speech recognition stage to improve its performance too, allowing it to fill in gaps where there is noise or ambiguity.

With the user's utterance duly parsed, the system can decide how to respond to it. Is it a request for information, or a command? Suppose it's a request for information. Is the information specific to the user, such as the time of a meeting or a friend's phone number, or is it an item of general knowledge? If it's a general knowledge question, then the system can call upon all the resources of the Internet to find an answer. The system can then transform the text of the answer into a sound file using speech synthesis technology that has been with us for many years (speech synthesis being much easier than speech recognition), and issue a verbal response through the device's speaker.

This is all very impressive. Admittedly, the conversational skills of a mid-2010s digital personal assistant are rather limited. You wouldn't invite one to a dinner party. But a generation ago, this sort of technology might have convinced a naïve user that we were well on the way to realizing the science fiction dream of artificial intelligence. And today, even knowing how they work, there is something uncanny about the capabilities of a personal assistant, an intimation of genuine intelligence. So what is missing? What would it take to convert this uncanny feeling, this intimation of intelligence, to well-founded conviction?

3.2 Getting to Know the World

A major shortcoming of these digital personal assistants is that they have no real knowledge of the world, despite their question-answering prowess. For example, they lack a commonsense understanding of solid objects and spatial relations. So they can be thrown by simple yet unexpected questions for which direct answers cannot be found on the Internet, vast as that repository is. For example, consider the question "If you dangle a rat by the tail, which is closer to the ground, its nose or its ears?" Even a child can solve this little riddle with ease. She may never have dangled a rat by its tail, nor seen a picture of a rat being dangled by its tail. Yet humans have a generic capability for visualizing situations and predicting the consequences of actions, a capability that can handle circumstances they have never previously encountered.

Everyday physics is one domain that humans (and some other animals) have properly mastered, a domain in which our grasp of the underlying principles enables us to solve problems quite unlike any we have seen before. Everyday psychology is another. Other people don't behave like inanimate objects. They have beliefs, desires, and intentions. Humans understand all this, and use this understanding to make plans, to communicate, and sometimes to deceive. For both these domains—everyday physics and everyday psychology—the depth of human understanding rests on the possession of a set of fundamental abstract concepts, such as that of a solid object or of another mind.

Although the neural mechanisms underlying these abilities in humans are not yet fully understood, it's safe to assume they are partly innate, an evolutionary endowment. Obviously solid objects and other people have always loomed large in the lives of hominids. General-purpose mechanisms for dealing with them will have been selected for. So even though the concept of a solid object is not manifest at birth, it would be surprising if the newborn brain were not predisposed to acquire it. Remarkably, though, humans are also able to acquire completely new concepts, concepts that are at least as abstract as that of a solid object or another mind and for which there is no precedent in our evolutionary past, such as the concept of an integer, or of money.

How can a machine be endowed with the same generic capacities—a mastery of important commonsense domains like everyday physics and everyday psychology, as well as the ability to acquire entirely new abstract concepts? One answer, of course, is to replicate the biological brain. But we have already discussed this at some length. There are several other possibilities. As far as everyday physics is concerned, one possibility is to employ a physics engine of the sort used in computer games and already discussed briefly in the context of virtual embodiment. A physics engine can model any given configuration of objects (e.g., the parts of a rat) and simulate their dynamics.

An alternative approach is to build a system that draws logical inferences about everyday things based on a set of laws of commonsense physics expressed in a formal language. For example, the system might contain a sentence representing the rule that unsupported objects normally fall down, and another that fragile objects normally break if they hit the ground. These could be used to draw the conclusion that a toppled wine glass will shatter if it rolls off a table. The same logic-based method can be applied to other domains, such as everyday psychology, and has the additional advantage over a physics engine of being more tolerant of incomplete information—about the exact shape of the table and the wine glass, for example.

However, both the physics engine and the logic-based approach are parasitic on conceptual frameworks provided by human designers. Information about a robot's environment—the surfaces of the objects around it—can be acquired by moving around, accumulating sensor data (from cameras, tactile sensors, etc.), and transforming the data into a form suitable for subsequent processing. But the very idea of a solid object, a concept that is vital to the predictive capabilities of either type of system, is not discovered through interaction with the world. It is given beforehand, built into the system from the start. This might be acceptable for some universally important domains of expertise (e.g., everyday physics), but a truly general intelligence also needs to be able to discover (or invent) abstract concepts for itself if it is to cope with a world that cannot be known in advance.

3.3 Machine Learning

This brings us to the topic of machine learning. Machine learning has been an active subfield of artificial intelligence since its inception. But the subject made considerable progress in the 2000s, thanks in part to increases in computing power and storage and in part to theoretical advances and new learning algorithms. This has led to novel commercial applications, such as online marketing, where it's useful to profile customers so as to more effectively target them with product recommendations and advertising. A machine learning system can do this by building a statistical model of customer behavior based on a large database of buying and browsing habits. With the aid of such a model the system can then predict the likely preferences of a customer based on just a few purchases and website visits.

Generally speaking, machine learning concerns the construction of a model that accounts for a given collection of data, and can be used to predict further data. For example, suppose I present you with the sequence 5, 10, 15, 20, and ask you to guess what comes next. The chances are you will form the hypothesis that the sequence increases in intervals of 5 and will predict that the next number is 25, followed by 30, 35, and so on. If the data have their origin in the real world, then the data are likely to be noisy. So machine learning algorithms have to be able to handle *uncertainty*. Suppose a mobile robot is stationary but is being approached by a large object. It obtains a series of sensor readings indicating the object's distance: 24.9 cm, 20.1 cm, 15.1 cm, 9.9 cm. It might form the hypothesis that the distance to the object decreases by approximately 5 cm per sensor reading, and predict that the next sensor reading will be 5.0 cm plus or minus 10 percent. Time to take evasive action!

In these trivial examples, spotting the underlying pattern is easy. But suppose that, instead of a single number, each item of data comprises a thousand numbers. Finding patterns, building models, and making predictions given high-dimensional data like these will be much harder. Indeed it's much worse than a thousand times harder. This is known as the *curse of dimensionality*. Thankfully though, the curse of dimensionality can be lifted to the extent that the data exhibit known statistical regularities. For

If the data have their origin in the real world, then the data are likely to be noisy. So machine learning algorithms have to be able to handle *uncertainty*.

example, suppose the data in question are a sequence of frames from a video. In this case there is a statistical tendency (1) for one pixel in any given frame to have a value close to that of its neighbors and (2) for the same pixel to have similar values in successive frames.

Statistical regularities like these are often a manifestation of the fundamental structure of the world from which the data are drawn. For a mobile robot with a camera, the world exhibits a kind of "smoothness." It is full of solid objects whose surfaces present lots of continuous patches of uniform color with relatively few discontinuous edges. Although some assumptions about the structure of the world might be built into a learning system at design time—such as its 3D spatial character and the prevalence within it of solid objects—much of the way the world is structured, the kinds of things it contains and the behavior they exhibit, will have to be discovered.

So the task of learning to predict incoming data by building a model of the world encompasses the challenge of finding ways to *compress* the data to reduce its dimensionality, for example, by re-describing it in terms of concepts and categories such as "animal," "tree," and "person" (which are also a useful foundation for linguistic communication). However, high-dimensional sensory data cannot be directly reduced to such high-level categories. A hierarchical approach is called for, wherein low-level features are extracted first. Having compiled a table of recurring low-level visual features, an algorithm can learn how those features combine to make higher level features. This multi-layered approach is the hallmark of so-called deep learning.

For example, suppose the learning algorithm was set to work on a large database of images, many of which contain faces. The presence of a face might be signaled by particular patterns of distinctively shaped patches of light and dark. These *might* correspond loosely to features we would call eyes, noses, and mouths. But they might not. The machine is not constrained by the categories of human language. The low-level, statistically significant visual features it picks out may not be amenable to straightforward linguistic description. (In fact the same is true of visual perception in the biological brain, although in humans it is subject to the top-down influence of language.)

Having learned the low-level statistics of the data—the small-scale visual motifs that recur over and again—the learning algorithm can learn that certain combinations of those motifs frequently arise. One such combination would correspond to what we would call a face. Another combination (whiskers, fur, pointy ears, etc.) might correspond to what we would call a cat. Or, since cats are frequently seen being cuddled by small humans, the algorithm might pick out child–cat pairings. Again, the machine is not constrained by human concepts and categories, just by the statistics of the data.

So far, so good. We have seen how a machine learning algorithm might work with *static* data. But what we're ultimately interested in is the *dynamics* of the world. We've been assuming a system that discovers categories of objects in a database of still images. But what about a video archive? After all, an embodied learning system needs to get to grips with moving images—indeed with an ever-flowing river of incoming sensory data—if it is to acquire predictive power. Moreover, for an AI with drives to satisfy and goals to achieve, it's only worth picking out the cats against the backdrop of the rest of the world to the extent that cats exhibit distinctive *behavior*, particularly if that behavior is relevant to the AI's drives and goals (as it would be for a mouse).

For example, if our learning algorithm had acquired the category "string" as well as the category "cat," then it would be half way to learning that cats often chase pieces of string. Once again, we shouldn't be misled into thinking that the way a machine learning algorithm would represent this rule would be anything like a sentence in human language. Rather, it would be a collection of parameter values within a data structure that captures the statistics of motion of certain frequently occurring visual features, which themselves would be represented in a similarly mathematical way. But the upshot would be the same for a suitably constructed machine as it would for a human who had learned this fact. It would, for example, put an AI in a good position to make a plan to lure a cat into a basket for transport to the vet.

3.4 AI through Big Data

Let's take stock. We've been discussing algorithms that can learn the statistics of the world, that can discover hierarchical categories of objects and behavior in an unlabeled stream of multimodal data, and that can use these categories to compress the data into a mathematical description that can be employed to make predictions. It's easy to see that machine learning algorithms of this sort constitute a useful technology. But how far do they take us toward artificial general intelligence?

Imagine an AI built along the following lines. Suppose a learning algorithm of the sort just described were allowed to crawl the Internet, like a search engine, sucking the statistics out of the billions of images, the tens of millions of videos it finds. Humanity has compiled a staggeringly large repository of multimedia data from the everyday world, and made it all accessible to anyone (or anything) with a network connection. Somewhere on the web are to be found movie clips of giraffes making love, of aircraft looping the loop, of men in India planting potatoes, of girls in China fixing bicycles, of battles, of board meetings, of building sites, and of cats charmingly doing very little. You name it, someone has probably taken a video of it and put it up on the web.

This public repository of data, already large, is growing rapidly thanks to the crowdsourcing power of social networking. Moreover much of it is more than just raw sensory data. Images and movie clips are typically accompanied by location, time, and date information, and increasingly by tags labeling objects and events. As more and more everyday objects become connected to the Internet (litter bins, fridges, key-rings, etc.), it will be possible to gather ever greater quantities of information about the everyday world and the behavior of the humans and other animals who inhabit it.

How good at prediction could a system become by applying powerful machine learning algorithms to this enormous repository of data? Why would the system need to be embodied? Why would it need to interact with the world directly, given an enormous database of multimedia recordings of the embodied activity of others? Recall that the difficulty of endowing a computer with a commonsense understanding of the everyday world has long been considered a major obstacle to achieving artificial general intelligence. Perhaps a disembodied AI could acquire common sense vicariously. How close could such a system get to human-level artificial intelligence?

Well, what about language? Language is a highly significant aspect of human behavior, and nothing could count as having attained human-level AI if it couldn't match human linguistic capability. The digital personal assistants of the mid-2010s are already uncannily good at anticipating what their users are about to say. But it's easy to argue that these systems don't really understand the words they recognize, the sentences they parse, or the answers they proffer. The symbols they use are not grounded in interaction with the world, a shortcoming that shows up when they are asked novel questions that require a combination of imagination and common sense: "If you dangle a rat by its tail, which is closer to the ground, its nose or its ears?"

Surely machine learning, however heavy-duty, cannot help us to overcome this sort of limitation? Yet language is just another form of behavior. Why should it be less susceptible to brute-force, statistical machine learning than, say, patterns of movement in a crowd or patterns of vegetation in a garden? Throw enough data and enough computation at the problem, and machine learning will be able to model the relevant statistics well enough to make reliable predictions. Where is this person likely to go having left the kiosk? What leaf shapes are likely to occur to the left of that tree? And what will this person say in response to what that person said? We mustn't forget that, compared to today's digital personal assistants, the sort of learning system we are envisaging will draw on a vastly larger dataset, one that effectively *does* ground words in experience, in embodied interaction with the world, albeit of a somewhat secondhand, parasitic kind.

What about the dangling rat example? Our AI needs to be able to deal with the hypothetical, the counterfactual, the imaginary. This is a basic piece of functionality. But given an adequate model of the world, a model with sufficient predictive power, all that is needed to fulfill this requirement is a means to initialize the model with hypothetical scenarios, a way of populating it with imaginary objects. The predictive power of the model will do the rest, generalizing from millions of videos of dangling things, tens of millions of images and videos of rats in a myriad poses doing a myriad things, and billions of examples of ears and noses from every conceivable angle.

How about, say, mathematics? Surely no mere statistical learning system could acquire the ability to do mathematics? (Students of philosophy will hear echoes of the debate between empiricism and rationalism here.) Well, we aren't ruling out supplying the system with various innate categories and concepts, such as that of a solid object or of 3D space. These could include the concept of number. But it isn't even clear that this is necessary. Perhaps it is enough for the learning algorithm to process a very large number of recordings of classroom lessons in primary school mathematics for it to discover the concept of number for itself. It's hard for us to imagine the implications of the sheer quantity of raw data the learning algorithm would have processed, and the ways in which the system might surprise us as a result.

In 2009 three computer scientists from Google wrote a paper entitled "The Unreasonable Effectiveness of Data."[1] The title alludes to an unexpected phenomenon in machine learning. It turns out that machine learning using a *messy* dataset with a *trillion* items can be highly effective in tasks (e.g., machine translation) for which machine learning using a *clean* dataset with a mere *million* items is downright useless. This is unexpected because a million seems like a big number. If a learning algorithm doesn't work with a training set comprising a million examples, then the intuitive conclusion is that it doesn't work at all. Yet it turns out that often what is needed is a much bigger training set, something that only came to light when computers became powerful enough to store and process that much data.

The lesson here is that when faced with artificial intelligence engineered from scratch, artificial intelligence that operates according to very different principles from the biological brain, we should expect to be surprised. In particular, if an AI system relies on quantities of data so large or processing speeds so fast that they are hard to grasp intuitively, then it might solve problems we don't expect it to solve in ways we don't fully understand. In short, human-level AI does not have to be human-like. If even human-level AI can be inscrutable, how could we hope to predict and control a superintelligent AI, a system capable not merely of matching humans in every domain of intellectual affairs but of outwitting us at every turn?

3.5 Optimization and Uncertainty

Of course, predictive capability does not alone constitute artificial general intelligence. Rather, the ability to build models of the world, and to use those models to make predictions, is a means to some other end. The intelligence of an animal is manifest in the things it does. It exhibits a sense of purpose. It has drives, such as hunger and fear, and it can form goals that subserve those drives, such as to acquire an item of food or to return home. It achieves its goals by acting on the world, and if it's clever, it will make predictions to help it achieve those goals. When our cat sees a mouse disappear behind a tree stump, it anticipates its reappearance, and waits patiently. We would expect the predictive capabilities of an embodied artificial general intelligence likewise to subserve goals and drives. It should display its own sense of purpose. Whether it was delivering parcels, cooking meals, or performing surgery, only if it had goals and were capable of achieving them would we think of a robot as possessing general intelligence.

If even human-level AI can be inscrutable, how could we hope to predict and control a superintelligent AI, a system capable not merely of matching humans in every domain of intellectual affairs but of outwitting us at every turn?

What about a disembodied AI? Well, even if its purpose were simply to answer questions and offer advice, to qualify as artificial general intelligence, a system would have to do more than just make predictions. Though incapable itself of acting directly on the world, it should be adept at working out how to act to achieve a variety of given aims. It might be asked to construct a profitable investment portfolio, or to plan a large civil engineering project, or to design a better drug, a larger aircraft, or a faster computer. If its intelligence were truly general, it would be possible to train it to do any (or all) of these things, as well as a host of others, just as it is with an intelligent human.

So what do we need over and above predictive capability to enable a machine, whether embodied or not, to carry out such challenging tasks? The AI needs to be able to *plan* a course of actions, and to be good at planning is to be good at a certain type of *optimization*. Indeed the topic of optimization is central to contemporary approaches to engineering artificial general intelligence from scratch. Not only can planning be cast as a form of optimization, so can certain kinds of machine learning and various aspects of computer vision, as well as many other problems relevant to artificial intelligence. So it's worth examining the concept in a little detail, which we'll do using a specific example, namely the *traveling salesperson problem*.

Suppose a traveler (or salesperson) is faced with the challenge of visiting a number of cities in turn, then returning home. She must visit each city exactly once and end up back where she started. But the order she chooses will influence her overall travel time, and she doesn't want to spend any longer on the road than she has to. Suppose she lives in San Francisco and has to visit New York, Boston, and San Jose. Because San Francisco and San Jose are near to each other but far from New York and Boston, it wouldn't make sense to go from San Francisco to New York then to San Jose and then to Boston before returning to San Francisco. That would be a suboptimal solution. The journey time will be shorter if she visits Boston right after New York. The challenge is to find the optimal solution, the best possible order in which to visit the cities, that is to say, the order that results in the shortest overall travel time.

The traveling salesperson problem is just one example of an optimization problem. In general, the task is to find some mathematically well-defined structure that minimizes some cost function (or, equivalently, that maximizes a so-called utility function or reward function). In this case the mathematical structure is an ordering of cities, and the cost function is the overall journey time. The problem doesn't look so hard with just a few cities to visit. But, like many optimization problems, the traveling salesperson problem doesn't scale well. In a specific mathematical sense (we won't go into the details) the difficulty of the problem goes up exponentially with the number of cities.

In effect this means that, with a large number of cities, even the fastest algorithm on the fastest conventional computer might struggle to find the optimal solution in a reasonable time. However, there are algorithms that will find a *good* solution for very large numbers of cities, although they may not find the *best possible* solution. This is fortunate because the traveling salesperson problem is more than just an intellectual curiosity. It has many practical applications, and usually finding a good solution is good enough.

Before we get back to artificial general intelligence, let's consider another optimization problem in which finding a good solution is good enough. Suppose that, instead of a traveling salesperson, we are dealing with our cat Tooty. Rather than visiting cities, Tooty's task, when he wakes up from a snooze, is to visit a number of local foraging sites, places where he often finds food (e.g., the neighbor's kitchen). Of course, moving from one such site to another takes up energy, and he would like to minimize the amount of energy he uses. He also wants to maximize his food intake. Annoyingly though, there is no guarantee that he will find food when he arrives at a foraging site. (The neighbor's cat might have got there first.) However, based on his past experience, Tooty "knows" the *probability* of finding food at any given site.

Now, the task for Tooty is to plan a tour of local foraging sites that will *maximize his expected reward*, where the reward he gains on each tour is some function of his total food intake and the energy he uses up. Unlike the traveling salesperson problem, the tour doesn't have to take in every site. So a good strategy might be to leave out distant, unpromising sites. Otherwise, this optimization task is quite similar to the traveling salesperson problem, and is computationally at least as hard. The main extra ingredient is *uncertainty*. However good a plan Tooty comes up with, there is no guarantee of how much food he will get. On a bad day, he might even get nothing.

But uncertainty is a fact of life. So a machine learning algorithm, however clever it is, cannot build a predictive model that will get it right every time. Instead, given finite, incomplete data, the best we can hope for is a *probabilistic* model, a model that can predict the most likely outcomes. Given a probabilistic model, the best course of action to pick is one that, according to the model, will maximize *expected* reward. However, we are still dealing with a well-specified optimization task. Uncertainty doesn't take us beyond the reach of mathematics and computation. It simply takes us into the mathematical realm of probability theory.

3.6   Universal Artificial Intelligence

Of course, a real cat wouldn't behave like the one in this caricature. The real Tooty doesn't wander around eating nothing while building a probabilistic model of his food supplies, then retire to his basket to work out an optimal route. Like any such well-adapted animal, a cat will learn while it forages, and forage while it learns. The business of exploring the world and the business of exploiting its resources are rolled into one. This is the right strategy, the rational strategy. As we will see, a similar strategy, one that interleaves machine learning and optimization, is a good basis for artificial general intelligence.

To AI researchers, the task of maximizing expected reward while trying out different actions in different situations to see which are the most effective is known as *reinforcement learning*. The traveling salesperson problem and the foraging cat problem are very specific examples of optimization. No algorithm that can only solve the traveling salesperson problem, however fast it might be, would constitute artificial general intelligence. By contrast, the idea of reinforcement learning, and the concept of maximizing expected reward that is central to it, are not tied down to particular problems. Indeed we can build on this idea to specify a form of *universal artificial intelligence*.[2]

The theoretical idea of universal artificial intelligence, which was first made precise by Marcus Hutter, is analogous to that of universal *computation*, one of Alan Turing's most important contributions to computer science. A universal computer is one that can compute anything that is possible to compute given the right program. Turing's achievement was to pin down the idea of such a computer mathematically. Unlike Turing's abstract computational devices (which we now call Turing machines), real computers are limited by finite memory. However, every digital computer that has ever been built can, in theory, compute anything that is possible to compute. They all inherit their generality from Turing's mathematical prescription.

Analogously, a universal artificial intelligence is one that always chooses an action that maximizes its expected reward given the information it has acquired, no matter what sort of world it finds itself in. It is, so to speak, a perfect AI, one whose decisions are guaranteed to make the most of its incoming data. Like Turing's notion of universal computation, this idea can be made mathematically precise. (We won't go into details here.) Also like Turing's notion, this mathematical ideal is not realizable in practice. Rather, it serves as a theoretical limit to the very idea of artificial intelligence, just as Turing's notion serves as a theoretical limit to the very idea of computation.

Despite its impracticality, the formal idea of universal artificial intelligence is more than a mathematician's plaything. To begin with, there are approximations to it that can be realized in practice. But the more relevant observation for the present discussion is that Hutter's mathematical characterization implies that artificial general intelligence conforms to a simple, generic architecture. This architecture interleaves two processes: machine learning, to construct probabilistic predictive models of the world, and optimization, to find actions that maximize expected reward according to those models.[3]

This two-component architectural blueprint has very wide application. Indeed any intelligent agent, whether artificial or biological, can be analyzed according to its structure. Three questions need to be asked (or three sets of questions). First, what is the agent's reward function? Answering this question will tell us a great deal about how it is likely to behave. Second, how does it learn? What data does it work with, what learning techniques does it use, and what prior knowledge of the world is built into them? Third, how does it maximize its expected reward? How powerful are the optimization techniques it uses to do this? What kinds of problems are they adept at solving, and what are their weaknesses and limitations?

Consider a nonhuman animal, such as a crow, which is capable of learning complex behaviors through trial and error, and also of a degree of innovative problem solving. What is its reward function? Like any animal, the reward function of a crow favors the acquisition of things like food and water while avoiding danger and discomfort. These might seem simple needs. But arbitrarily complex problems can be presented in the guise of barriers to obtaining food.

For example, to test a crow's cognitive abilities, a researcher might present it with a worm in a box whose lid can only be opened by solving a puzzle. Crows, which are particularly clever animals, can solve simple planning problems presented this way. But trickier problems could be given the same form. For example, a less fortunate crow might be obliged to win a game of chess to get the lid open. This crow would no doubt go hungry. But the point is that the imperative to obtain a resource like food can be thought of as a *universal reward function*. In a complex environment the class of problems that can be translated into the challenge of gaining a simple resource is open-ended.

So much for the first question, the question of reward function. The next question to ask is how the crow learns. The crow learns from data that pours in through its senses, thanks to its embodied interaction with the physical world, a world that manifests numerous objects, both animate and inanimate, with a rich variety of shapes and dynamics. The crow learns how these objects behave when pushed, poked, pecked, or squawked at, or when simply left alone. Precisely how it does this, what the neural underpinnings of this process are, is a scientific question we haven't yet answered. But animal cognition researchers have given us a good idea of the kinds of associations that animals like crows can form, the sorts of sensory discriminations they can make, and so on.

How good is a crow at finding actions that maximize its expected reward? The answer, in the case of the crow, is better than most animals. It has a rich underlying repertoire of actions, one that that includes tool use. These form the basis of a number of innate stimulus–response behaviors that are evolution's contribution of useful prior assumptions about the world to the crow's reward-maximizing powers. But a crow does more than simply rely on a lookup table that maps stimulus to response (which is enough even for tool use). It can find new sequences of actions to solve previously unseen problems, sometimes innovating new kinds of behaviors (e.g., manufacture a novel tool). Again, the neural underpinnings of this ability have yet to be revealed. But the crow's optimization method, whatever it is, appears to be very general, very powerful, at least compared to other nonhuman animals.

All this tells us a great deal about the capacities and limitations of crows, and helps us predict their behavior. We know, for example, that a crow might upset a rubbish bin to get access to food scraps. But we needn't worry that it will hack into a bank account and steal our money. To better understand the capacities and limitations of different kinds of artificial intelligence, we can ask the same questions. What are the implications of different sorts of reward functions? What kinds of machine learning techniques might an AI be equipped with? What data will they work with? What kinds of optimization algorithms might be deployed to maximize an AI's expected reward?

3.7 Human-Level and Human-Like Intelligence

Crows, like chimpanzees, dogs, elephants, and many other nonhuman animals, are impressively clever. But they are far less clever than humans. Animal-level AI would be useful. A robot with the intelligence of a dog, say, could perform a range of worthwhile tasks. But our real concern here is human-level artificial general intelligence. We would like to know how an AI might be built that can match a typical human in almost every sphere of intellectual activity, and maybe surpass the typical human in some. Or at least we would like to form a sufficient idea of how such an AI would work to imagine what the future might be like if it contained such machines. Then we can begin to think through the possibility of superintelligent AI, of artificial intelligence capable of *outwitting* humans in every sphere of intellectual activity.

Whether we're thinking about a human-level AI or a superintelligent AI, we need to ask the same three questions as before: What is its reward function? How and what does it learn? How does it optimize for expected reward? But before we embark on this imaginative exercise, it's instructive to ask the same questions of *homo sapiens*. First, what is the human reward function? Well, we surely have roughly the same *underlying* reward function as other animals. Humans need food and water, prefer not to be in pain, enjoy sex, and so on. Moreover the human reward function is "universal," like the crow's: any intellectual challenge could, in theory, be presented to a human being in the guise of gaining food, say, or sex. Significantly, though, humans seem capable of radically *modifying* their reward functions.

Many animal species will learn to associate objects or events with reward, as in the famous example of Pavlov's dog, who learned to associate the sound of a bell with the arrival of food after repeatedly being presented with both stimuli together. Eventually the dog would begin to salivate upon hearing the bell even in the absence of food. This sort of conditioning is useful for maximizing expected reward. In a competitive setting the dog that runs to its bowl when it hears the bell will get more food than the dog that is ignorant of the correlation. But in such cases the underlying reward function hasn't really changed. It remains firmly grounded in the biological fundamentals.

In humans, by contrast, the layering of associations one upon another from childhood onward, mediated by complex social cues and expectations, can result in an apparent disconnect between reward function and biology. Indeed it might even be argued that part of the essence of our humanity is the capacity to transcend the contingencies of biology. Humans play music, write poems, design gardens, and so on. No doubt such activities are often pursued for financial gain or for social status, motives that might be explained in terms of biological imperatives. But sometimes they are surely the outcome of reflection on what constitutes a good life, and thereby become ends in themselves rather than merely a surrogate for obtaining food or avoiding danger or anything else with obvious evolutionary value.

This brings us to the question of how humans learn about the world, and whether there is anything distinctive about what humans learn compared to other animals. The answer is obvious. The open-endedness of the human reward function is made possible thanks to society, to culture, but above all to *language*. It is thanks to language that we can reflect on the human condition, as we do in philosophy, art, and literature. Without such reflection it's hard to see how we could overcome biological imperatives to the extent that we seemingly do. It's also thanks to language that humans are able to cooperate in the development of technology, and that the fruits of one generation's technological labors can be passed on so easily to the next. So, besides learning about the everyday physical, natural, and social world, the human must be able to learn language. A predisposition to understand the minds of others in terms of their beliefs, desires, emotional states, and so on, helps make the business of learning tractable here.

Finally, how do humans maximize expected reward? Once again, society, culture, and language are prominent here. Human intelligence is collective. Not only is human technology the product of many individuals and their labors, it is the product of many generations of individuals. Knowledge, expertise, and infrastructure accrete layer by layer, each generation building on the achievements of the one before. So the optimizing powers of the individual human are specialized for maximizing reward within a society. It makes no difference whether an individual's reward function is admirable or despicable, whether a person is a saint or a sinner. A human must work out how to get what she wants from other people, given the society she finds herself in and calling on the resources of its language to do so.

Whether operating collectively or individually, the capacity to innovate is another key element of the human strategy for optimizing reward. (Recall that endowing a computer with creativity was cited as a major obstacle to achieving artificial general intelligence in chapter 1.) The inventions of agriculture, writing, printing, the steam engine, the computer, and so on, have all contributed enormously to human health, life expectancy, and general well-being, and thereby helped maximize reward over a long timescale. In addition to favoring good health and longevity, the human reward function has been shaped by sexual selection, competition for social status, and other peculiarly biological factors. The result is the less obviously utilitarian forms of creativity exemplified by dance, ritual, fashion, art, music, and literature.

Now, what would a human-level AI engineered from scratch be like? To what extent must the three key questions—the questions of reward function, learning, and optimization—have answers for this sort of AI that resemble those for a human being? Well, if an AI is to be human-*like*, it should broadly conform to the pattern set out above, even if its design and construction bear no resemblance to the human brain. However, as we already noted in the context of the "unreasonable effectiveness of data," there is no reason for human-level artificial intelligence to be human-like. As long as the AI can match the typical human in most spheres of intellectual activity, and maybe surpass the typical human in a few, its intelligence would qualify as human-level.

This leaves a lot of room for variation, just as we find plenty of variation within the human population. Some people are good with numbers, others are good with words. Some people are people people, others are more at home with technology. Similarly a human-level artificial general intelligence might have a very large working memory capacity or be highly skilled at searching for patterns in data, yet be incapable of writing a worthwhile novel or of devising a new musical form (as are most humans). But what if an artificial intelligence had some ability that enabled it not merely to match humans but to outwit them in every sphere of intellectual activity? Is such a superintelligent machine possible? What would be the consequences of creating it? These are among the questions to be tackled in the next chapter.

SUPERINTELLIGENCE

4.1 Toward Superintelligence

We now have an overview of various enabling technologies, some biologically inspired, others the result of engineering from scratch, that could contribute to the creation of artificial general intelligence at the human level and beyond. The elements that can be made using these enabling technologies might be thought of as a set of building blocks that can be assembled in different combinations to make a variety of forms of artificial intelligence. To gain some understanding of what the resulting systems might be capable of and how they might behave, we can use the framework of three questions proposed in the previous chapter. What is the system's reward function? How and what does it learn? How does it optimize for expected reward?

We can also begin to ask a number of more philosophical questions. Would it be capable of moral judgments, and should it therefore be held responsible for its actions? Would it be capable of suffering, and should it therefore have rights? How much freedom to act should it be afforded? Finally, we can begin to question the consequences for society, for humanity as a whole, of introducing such systems into the world. If their freedom to act were not curtailed, how and to what extent would they reshape our world? What impact would they have on our economy, on our social fabric, on our sense of what it means to be human? What kind of world would result? Would the arrival of such machines lead to a utopia, to a dystopia, or would it leave things much as they are?

Before exploring these issues in detail, we need to examine a critically important proposition. The proposition is that if and when human-level AI is achieved, superintelligent AI will be almost inevitable. To see the plausibility of this claim, we only need to consider the advantages of implementation in a digital rather than biological substrate. Unlike a biological brain, a digitally realized brain emulation can be copied arbitrarily many times. And unlike a biological brain, a digital brain can be speeded up. So, if we can create one human-level AI by whole brain emulation, then, given sufficient computational resources, we can create a community of many such human-level AIs, all working at superhuman speeds. The same point can be made for AI that has been engineered from scratch. Indeed anything realized as a computer program can be copied and/or accelerated.

Unlike a biological brain, a digitally realized brain emulation can be copied arbitrarily many times. And unlike a biological brain, a digital brain can be speeded up.

The implications of this are far-reaching. To make these implications more vivid, let's imagine a concrete scenario. Suppose a major corporation with a famous brand name decides to develop a new high-performance motorbike in response to projected demand in emerging markets. The corporation awards contracts to two automotive design companies to come up with prototypes. The best prototype will go to manufacture (and earn the designers lots of money). One company employs a traditional team of human designers. The other company is a start-up that builds specialist teams of human-level AIs who inhabit virtual environments where they are set to work on large-scale design projects such as this.

The project requires expertise in many areas, including materials, engine design, fluid dynamics, and ergonomics, as well as a talent for knowing what looks good. From concept to first working prototype is expected to take a top-notch (human) team two years. The AI-based design company seems to be at a distinct disadvantage. They have no automotive design experts on the payroll. However, they have enormous computing resources and the latest AI technology on their side. So assembling a crack team of designers from scratch is no problem.

They start by populating a virtual world with a set of off-the-shelf apprentice AIs. These are human-level artificial intelligences that come pre-loaded with the acquired experience of an average human in their early twenties plus a graduate-level education in some relevant field such as mechanical engineering or industrial design. Now, this group of apprentices isn't going to cut it as an automotive design team. Their human rivals in the other company have all had years of industrial experience designing cars, bikes, and engines. To get up to speed, the AI team will have to acquire comparable experience. Fortunately, they can do this in their virtual world, completing a plethora of mini projects, some as individuals, some as a team.

Of course, if this training had to take place in real time, the virtual team would get nowhere. Their human rivals would produce a prototype bike before the AI team was in a position to get started. But suppose the AIs operate ten times faster than real time. Then ten years of training and design experience could be compressed into just twelve months. By the start of year two of the project, the AI team will have caught up with the human team. Moreover they will have ten years of subjective time ahead of them to come up with the perfect superbike, compared to just one year remaining for their biologically constrained human counterparts. Just imagine what a group of talented, enthusiastic young human engineers might accomplish in ten years.

So the second year of the project elapses, and the rival teams submit their designs to the contractors. The traditional design company have produced a fine prototype bike, sleek and elegant, sure to appeal to the target market.

But what about the AI-based company? When they unveil their prototype, everyone is astonished. No one has seen a bike quite like it before. But if the look is nothing short of revolutionary, the specifications defy belief. How is it possible to get such acceleration and such a top speed with such low fuel consumption?

Having been declared winners, the AI team can reveal some of their secrets. With so much time on their hands, they were able to develop a whole new range of biomaterials perfectly suited to motorbike manufacture, and a miniature fuel preprocessing plant that uses some previously unexploited results from chemistry. Additionally they managed to develop a fabrication method that allows all the bike's electronics to be integrated into its frame and manufactured all at once, in one piece. All these technologies have been duly patented, and promise to earn the design company a fortune besides the earnings from their winning bike design.

The lesson of this little story is that if and when human-level AI is achieved, superintelligence will soon follow. It doesn't require the creation of a new form of intelligence. It doesn't require a conceptual breakthrough. Even if human-level AI is achieved by the most conservative means—by slavishly copying nature—the resulting liberation from the speed restrictions inherent in biology is enough. But is this really superintelligence? After all, by hypothesis, there is nothing that a team of accelerated human brain emulations could achieve that couldn't be achieved by a team of humans, given enough time.

Well, maybe a distinction could be drawn between individual superintelligence and collective superintelligence. What we have in this story seems to be a form of *collective* superintelligence. No *individual* member of the AI team meets the criterion of superintelligence. None, by itself, is capable of systematically outwitting the average human being. However, the individual/collective distinction makes little difference in a discussion of the potential consequences of developing superintelligent AI. It would be no consolation to the losing design team to know they were defeated by a collective rather than a brilliant individual. Likewise, if humanity is ultimately delivered either into a utopia or a dystopia thanks to the creation of human-level AI, no one will care whether the culprit is "proper" superintelligence or not.

In the end, what matters is what the technology is able to do. The science fiction writer Arthur C. Clarke famously remarked that "any sufficiently advanced technology is indistinguishable from magic." Human-level AI, however it is achieved, is likely to lead directly to technology that, to the rest of us, will be indistinguishable from magic. All it requires is faster computation, as the motorbike story shows. But to see the truly disruptive potential of reaching this milestone, we must factor in other possible ways of improving the capabilities of human-level AI. These will depend on the nature of the underlying technology. In due course we will look at the prospect of superintelligence via AI engineered from scratch. But first, let's focus on brain-inspired human-level AI.

4.2 Brain-Inspired Superintelligence

In the story of the motorbike designers, the team of AIs has an enormous competitive advantage over their human rivals simply by working very fast. If the AIs in question were brain-like, this would amount to their operating in faster than real time. This is the simplest and most obvious way to exploit the liberation from biological constraints that results from migration to a computational substrate. But the migration from biology opens up many more possibilities for enhancing the capabilities of brain-inspired artificial intelligence.

Consider all the ways in which human workers are hampered by their animal nature. Humans need to eat, for example, and to sleep. But even a biologically highly realistic whole brain emulation—a faithful synthetic copy of a specific brain—could to a large extent be relieved of these needs. While real brains require a blood supply to provide energy, in the form of glucose, to enable neurons to function, a simulated brain has no such requirements, at least not at the level of the simulation. (Obviously the computers running the simulation would require energy, but this is a separate issue.) Sleep is more complex, since dreaming seems to serve an important psychological function. So in a whole brain emulation, it might not be a straightforward matter simply to eliminate the need for sleep. Nevertheless, a designer brain—one based on the principles of operation of the vertebrate nervous system but not conforming to the brain of any living species— could perhaps be carefully engineered not to require sleep.

In short, a brain-inspired human-level AI wouldn't have to waste time finding food, preparing it, and eating it. Nor would it have to spend time (or as much time, in the case of whole brain emulation) unproductively asleep. The time duly saved could be devoted to work, and the resulting increase in its effective workload would confer the same sort of advantage as acceleration, albeit on a less dramatic scale. Of course, most humans would object to having their mealtimes and their sleep replaced by work. But the reward function of a designer brain could be tuned differently. A willing intellectual slave who never eats or sleeps and wants nothing more than to work would be many corporations' idea of the perfect employee, espe- cially if they don't require wages.

Eliminating the need for food and sleep is one straight- forward way to exploit the liberation from biology. Other relatively conservative techniques for getting the most out of brain-inspired AI are easy to imagine. Many humans enhance their cognitive performance using the tried-and-tested pharmaceutical trick of caffeine ingestion. Hallucinogens such as psilocybin (the active ingredient in magic mushrooms) have often been claimed to promote creativity, their legal status notwithstanding. In a simulated brain the effects of such drugs can themselves be simulated, without any unwanted side effects on the rest of the body. Moreover there's no need to stick to pharmaceutically realistic interventions. With innumerable easily modified parameters, there would be a myriad ways to beneficially modulate the activity of a simulated brain, and thereby to optimize it for a particular task.

Somewhat less conservatively, there are various ways a simulated brain might be enhanced at the anatomical level, along lines already envisaged in chapter 2 when considering how a mouse-scale whole brain emulation might be upgraded to human-level intelligence. For example, it might be possible to enlarge the prefrontal cortex, simply by adding to its neuron count. This would be relatively straightforward in a computer simulation, where the brain doesn't have to fit inside a physical cranium. The prefrontal cortex is heavily implicated in working memory, an essential component of high-level cognition, and humans have markedly larger prefrontal cortices than other primates. So a superhumanly large prefrontal cortex could be highly advantageous. Similar enlargements can be envisaged for other regions, such as the hippocampus, which is involved in long-term memory.

At the collective level, there are other methods for increasing the capabilities of a team of brain-based human-level AIs. Unlike a wetware brain, it's easy to make multiple copies of a simulated brain. This opens up various possibilities for exploiting parallelism that are not available to a biological brain. Suppose an AI is attempting to solve some problem, and several distinct ways of approaching the problem present themselves. Then, rather than trying each possibility, one at a time in serial order, several copies of the AI can be made and each set to work on one of the possibilities, thus enabling many avenues to be explored at once. When all of the copies have finished trying out their particular approach, the most successful can be chosen.

To pick a simple example, suppose an AI is playing a game of chess. From the board's current configuration, there are three promising moves for the AI. It could explore each move in turn, one at a time. But alternatively, three copies of the AI can be spawned, one to investigate each move. When all three have looked as far ahead in the game as they can, their results are pooled, and the best move is chosen. The extra copies of the AI would then need to be destroyed (terminated), leaving just one to make the selected move and continue with the game. This type of parallelism is widely used in computer science today, to great effect. So the idea of spawning multiple copies of a simulated brain is just an extension of a tried-and-tested programming technique.

Perhaps the most potent factor in the likely development of superintelligence, whether we're talking about brain-based AI or AI engineered from scratch, is the prospect of *recursive self-improvement*. The idea is straightforward. A human-level AI is, by definition, capable of matching humans in almost every sphere of intellectual activity. One such sphere of intellectual activity is the construction of artificial intelligence. A first generation human-level artificial intelligence would be in much the same position as the human engineers that created it. Both species of engineer, biological and artificial, might call upon techniques like those just discussed to boost intelligence. However, the next generation of AIs, those whose intelligence is slightly above human level, will be better at engineering AI than any human.

A sufficiently brilliant human neuroscientist could open up whole new vistas of theory, unearthing principles we can hardly imagine today, with far-reaching implications for neural engineering and brain-based artificial intelligence. A team of brilliant artificially intelligent neuroscientists working at superhuman speeds, or otherwise exploiting the possibilities afforded by liberation from biology, would be even more effective. They would be in a position to produce the next generation of brain-based AIs more rapidly than the previous generation was produced by its human developers. Each successive generation would appear more quickly than the last, following a quintessentially exponential curve. The result would be a sort of *intelligence explosion*.[1]

4.3 Optimization and Creativity

So far in this chapter we have largely concentrated on human-like artificial intelligence. But human-like intelligence probably occupies just a small patch in the space of possible AIs. Now we'll shift our attention to other possibilities, and it will be important to shed any anthropomorphizing tendencies along the way. It's reasonable to hope that the behavior of an AI based on the vertebrate brain will be comprehensible to us on some level, even if it is accelerated, parallelized, or enhanced toward superintelligence. There is much less reason to assume this for an AI engineered from scratch. We should expect to be baffled and to be surprised, perhaps pleasantly, perhaps unpleasantly.

How might superintelligence arise in a system that was engineered from scratch, a system whose design has no biological counterpart? We get a glimpse of a possible answer by appealing to the three-part framework introduced in chapter 3. When it comes to engineering artificial intelligence from scratch, this framework is prescriptive rather than merely descriptive. According to the prescription, artificial general intelligence can be realized by (1) devising the right reward function, (2) implementing an effective learning technique to build a model of the world, and (3) deploying a powerful optimization method capable of maximizing expected reward given that learned model.

To get a feel for what might be achieved with this simple architectural specification, let's revisit the central issue of creativity. At first, it's hard to see how any sort of innovation or novelty could emerge from the combination of machine learning and optimization. Surely these processes are forever condemned to operate with a fixed set of raw ingredients—cities and journeys in the traveling salesman problem, for example. How could they possibly come up with a completely new concept, such as farming, or writing, or postmodernism, or punk rock? But to see how misleading this intuition is we need only consider the example of evolution by natural selection.

From an algorithmic point of view, evolution by natural selection is remarkably simple. Its basic elements are replication, variation, and competition, each repeated countless times. Computationally speaking, it exploits staggeringly massive parallelism and has to run for a very long time before doing anything interesting. But astonishingly, it has generated all complex life on Earth. It has done this through sheer brute force and without recourse to reason or explicit design. Along the way, it came up with such marvels as the hand, the eye, and the brain. In turn, the brain (along with the hand and the eye) came up with farming, writing, postmodernism, and punk rock.

Now, it isn't quite right to describe evolution by natural selection as an optimization process. Although evolution can be thought of as the by-product of many competing genes trying to maximize their proliferation, there is no global cost function or utility function guiding its progress. However, just like an optimization process, evolution explores a vast space of possibilities. To solve the traveling salesperson problem requires a search through the (relatively small) space of possible city tours, whereas evolution explores the (much larger) space of possible organisms. In contrast to the traveling salesperson problem, where journey time guides the search, evolution explores blindly. But despite this lack of direction, and despite its inherent simplicity, evolution has produced solutions to problems that would challenge any general intelligence, such as solar energy storage and heavier-than-air flight.

What this shows is that creativity can emerge from a simple process like optimization. But it does require a special sort of optimization. Computer scientists have devised many algorithms for solving the traveling salesperson problem, but none of those algorithms is going to invent the hand or the eye on its way to finding a good solution. The most important prerequisite for a creative process concerns the raw ingredients it works with. These must be amenable to *open-ended recombination*, like Lego bricks, which is to say, it must be possible to assemble them in different ways to produce an endless variety of things. Evolution by natural selection meets this criterion, thanks to the chemical properties of the organic molecules that are the basis of life. An optimization method could meet the same criterion if its raw ingredients were, say, designs for submission to a 3D printer, or virtual objects in a physics-based simulator, or the organic chemistry set of real or synthetic biology.

The second feature required by an optimization process if it is to be capable of creativity is a *universal reward function*. A reward function that is too easily satisfied will not promote novelty. Creativity is of no benefit to a male redback spider whose only task is to deliver a genetic load to a receptive female. Having fully satisfied his life's mission, the male spider can allow himself to be cannibalized by his mate. By contrast, in a sufficiently rich environment, the challenge of acquiring a resource such as food or money might require the solution of any problem it is possible to devise. In a competitive context where there is not enough of the resource to go round, ingenuity may be required just to survive. And where there is an incentive to amass as much of a resource as possible, the potential for creativity is endless.

Finally, to exhibit creativity, the optimization algorithm must be powerful enough. Possessing a universal reward function and working with raw ingredients amenable to open-ended recombination will not lead to anything noteworthy if the optimization algorithm confines its search to a small, tried-and-tested portion of the space of possibilities. Rather, it needs to carry out a *playful* exploration of the space of possibilities. It has to try out new combinations of the raw ingredients it has available in order to invent new things. Indeed it has to be able to invent whole new categories of useful things, such as books, steam engines, and websites. It has to be able to invent whole new technologies.

This doesn't sound anything like the sort of optimization algorithm contemporary computer science students learn about, the kind of thing that can solve the traveling salesperson problem. Surely an optimization algorithm that powerful would be so sophisticated, so complicated that we can barely imagine how it would work today, just as today we have only the barest understanding of how intelligence is realized in the human brain. But recall the lesson of evolution by natural selection. Advanced technology can emerge from even a simple, brute-force algorithm, given enough time. If we devised the right sort of simple, brute-force optimization algorithm, supplied it with an open-ended reward function, and unleashed it in an environment with enough combinatorial potential, then the only thing limiting its capabilities would be computing power.

So this suggests a way of building artificial general intelligence using brute-force search with massive amounts of computing power. But in an important sense, the resulting system wouldn't possess genuine intelligence.

It wouldn't investigate the world and build up scientific knowledge. It wouldn't construct rational arguments. Nothing it produced would be the result of analyzing a problem or applying principles of design. Rational enquiry and principled design make intelligence a dramatically more efficient approach to developing new technology than brute-force search. In nature, the brute-force approach has bootstrapped its way to intelligence by evolving the brain. But the goal of AI research is to endow systems with intelligence directly.

Supplementing playful, undirected search with rational enquiry and principled, goal-directed design dramatically shortcuts the slow process of trial and error and compensates for limited computing power. So we should expect these functions to be part of a truly powerful optimization algorithm, one capable of creativity. But they rely on having a model of the world, a way to predict the outcome of actions or the efficacy of a novel design. This is where machine learning comes in—and where the analogy with evolution breaks down. If evolution were trying to maximize a reward function, we would count it as very inefficient. Like a bad scientist, it throws away all its data. It doesn't use the results of its experiments in organism design to build a model of the world whose predictions can inform subsequent design decisions.

But evolution has no reward function, no global utility function. From an evolutionary standpoint, there is only one way to judge an alteration to body shape or a variation in behavior: that is to try it out in the competitive struggle to survive and reproduce. So it makes no sense to find fault with evolution in this respect. By contrast, the sort of AI we are envisaging here is trying to maximize its expected reward. In the context of a reward function, an effective strategy is to test out ideas (designs) in theory or in simulation before they are deployed in practice, to "look before leaping." To do this, a model of the world is needed, and machine learning is required to construct and maintain this model, whether through embodied interaction with a physical and social environment or vicariously via the Internet.

4.4 Engineering Superintelligence

The take-home message of the previous section is that even a crude optimization algorithm may be enough for human-level AI given sufficient computing power. Even creativity, one the most difficult qualities to realize in a computer, can emerge from a brute-force search if enough processing time is available. But if (as we might expect) the enormous computing power required is beyond the reach of Moore's law, then the shortfall can be made up by endowing the AI with sophisticated cognitive capacities— rational enquiry, principled design, theoretical analysis, and simulation. Very well, let's suppose this is sufficient to achieve human-level AI by the engineering route (as opposed to the brain-inspired route). What about going beyond human-level intelligence? Can superintelligence be achieved this way?

The first thing to note is that AI developers who take the engineering route can avail themselves of the two main tricks that made the transition from human-level to superhuman-level intelligence seem feasible for a brain-based AI, namely speedup and parallelism. If a developer has the knowledge and computing power to engineer an AI with human-level intelligence, then all it needs to build a collaborative team of accelerated versions of the same AI is more computing power (assuming the nature of the AI didn't somehow prevent it from working in a team). As we saw in the example of the motorbike design challenge, this would be enough to yield a collective intelligence that, to the outside world, would appear superhumanly capable. As with brain-based AI, once an AI is engineered whose intelligence is only slightly above human level, the dynamics of recursive self-improvement become applicable, potentially triggering an intelligence explosion.

The engineering approach to artificial general intelligence might even bypass human-level AI altogether, and achieve a form of superintelligence in one fell swoop. Indeed there are several ways this could happen. Before delving into this possibility, though, a few words are in order on the very idea of a scale of intelligence. According to the definition we've been using, an AI possesses human-level intelligence if it can match the performance of an average human in all, or nearly all, spheres of intellectual activity. If it can outwit human beings at every turn, then it is superintelligent. Interpolating here, it's tempting to assume a neat, well-ordered scale of intelligence. The mouse is at one end, the human a little further along, and the superintelligent AI further along still. Given such a scale, it makes sense to speak putatively of an AI that is 10 times as intelligent as a human, or even 100 times as intelligent.

However, this assumes a very coarse-grained notion of intelligence. In humans, intelligence manifests as a patchwork of skills, and different individuals have different strengths and weaknesses. Someone who is highly artistic may be weak at mathematics, while another person who is a brilliant writer might have a poor understanding of music. Now that we're dealing with forms of artificial intelligence that diverge radically from the human archetype, it is especially important to be sensitive to this point. Even in the context of general intelligence, we should expect a system to exhibit a pattern of cognitive strengths and weaknesses, rather than a single, monolithic property of (super)intelligence. In other words, the same AI might be superhumanly clever in some respects but surprisingly deficient in others.

Now, an AI that was sufficiently capable in one domain could compensate for its weaknesses in others. We find the same thing in humans. People with dyslexia, for example, often find very effective coping strategies for dealing with the challenge of reading. Similarly an AI that, say, lacked the rhetorical skills to persuade humans to invest in a business proposal that it had devised could use different means (e.g., brilliantly playing the stock market) to achieve the same end of raising money. More generally, a system employing a very powerful optimization process combined with a very powerful machine learning algorithm applied to a very large amount of data might find ways to maximize expected reward that we can barely imagine.

Of course, however good it was at chess, an AI that was constitutionally incapable of dealing with anything other than chess positions wouldn't be able to achieve much. To qualify as having general intelligence, the *cognitive purview* of the AI must be comparable to that of a human. Not only can humans perceive, act on, think about, and talk about the contents of the everyday world (cats, teacups, buses, etc.), they can also imagine stars, galaxies, cells, and atoms, as well as unicorns, magnetic fields, computer programs, and bank accounts. We can (learn to) think and talk about all these things, and can imagine manipulating them all to our ends (if only we were large enough, or small enough, or had the right sorts of tools).

But there is a distinction between *purview* and *performance*. A good analogy here is the triathlon in athletics. To take part in a triathlon, an athlete has to be able to run, to swim, and to ride a bike. All three skills must be in within the athlete's physical purview, so to speak. But an athlete's performance can differ from one event to another. And an athlete who is especially strong in one event can compensate for his or her deficiencies in the others. Likewise the cognitive purview of an artificial general intelligence must encompass all the kinds of things that humans can perceive, act on, think about, and talk about. But its performance can vary from one kind of intellectual activity to another. And its weaknesses in one domain can be made up for by strengths in another.

With this distinction between purview and performance in mind, let's return to the possibility of an AI attaining superintelligence without passing through the stage of human-level intelligence. For the kind of AI we've been envisaging here to have an adequate cognitive purview, one that would allow its performance to match humans in (almost) every sphere of intellectual activity, it would need to employ an especially powerful combination of optimization process and machine learning algorithm, a combination that incorporated a commonsense understanding of the world and from which creativity could emerge. Since the human brain broadly fits this description, there is good reason to think that such a combination is possible, even if it deviates from the human brain in its architecture.

Now, here is the important point. In order for a system to attain a cognitive purview comparable to that of a human by means of powerful optimization and learning, it might already have to be capable of superhuman cognitive performance in certain respects. In particular, consider a disembodied system that applies machine learning to the very large quantities of data available on the Internet—or rather on the Internet of the future. As well as real-time information broadcast on social and other media and enormous historical repositories of text, images, and movie clips, it will be able to draw on data from a vast network of pervasive sensors, in portable and wearable devices, in vehicles, indeed in everything from street furniture to toasters.

The human brain is good at finding patterns in high bandwidth data from a very specific, spatially localized source, namely the sensory apparatus attached to the body. This is fine from an evolutionary standpoint because, above all else, an animal needs to be able to deal with the things it can see, hear, and touch in order to find food, to avoid predators, to rear young, and so on. The human brain isn't bad at finding patterns in other kinds of data too, such as stock market trends, ecosystem dynamics, or the weather. But this sort of data comes to it indirectly, translated into terms that its spatially localized senses can handle, such as words, pictures, and formulas.

The sort of AI we are envisaging here will also be adept at finding patterns in large quantities of data. But unlike the human brain, it won't be expecting that data to be organized in the distinctive way that data coming from an animal's senses are organized. It won't depend on the distinctive spatial and temporal organization of that data, and it won't have to rely on associated biases, such as the tendency for nearby data items to be correlated (e.g., nearby patches of color often move in the same way across the visual field because they are frequently on the surface of the same object). To be effective, the AI will need to be able to find and exploit statistical regularities without such help, and this entails that it will be very powerful and very versatile.

So—to pick out one sphere of intellectual activity—the AI is likely to be very good at interpreting, predicting, and manipulating human behavior, not necessarily on an individual scale but on a mass social scale. Its access to the relevant data, harvested from the Internet and elsewhere, will be direct and unmediated, like the human brain's access to what can be seen, heard, or touched. This unmediated access is likely to confer a decisive advantage over human intelligence in many domains. Scientific discovery in fields such as genetics and neuroscience, for example, is increasingly dependent on big data, a trend that is likely to continue into the coming decades. An AI that is designed from the outset to find patterns in large volumes of data will immediately be superhumanly capable in such fields.

4.5   User Illusion or Anthropomorphism?

Another cognitive function where engineered AIs would have an inbuilt advantage over their biological progenitors is communication. As the philosopher Ludwig Wittgenstein made clear, language has a multitude of uses in human society. But one of its roles is the communication of beliefs, desires, and intentions. In a novel, a poem, or a play, ambiguity and a certain openness to multiple readings are a virtue. But in science and technology, precision is paramount. The members of a team working toward a scientific or technological goal need to be able to communicate their beliefs, desires, and intentions unambiguously. While humans have to translate their thoughts into the noisy, low-bandwidth medium of language, a team of AIs could in principle transmit their beliefs, desires, and intentions clearly and directly to one another.

Moreover the very idea of a collective of AIs analogous to a human team is open to challenge when we depart from the blueprint of the biological brain. The idea of a team presupposes that each AI is a separate entity that can be clearly individuated. But for a computer system, identity is a more fluid notion than it is in biology. There are many ways that a complex, massively parallel system realized on distributed hardware and software might be divided and subdivided into parts. The concept of an individual artificial intelligence might be less appropriate than that of an amorphous, ambient artificial intelligence.

The concept of an individual artificial intelligence might be less appropriate than that of an amorphous, ambient artificial intelligence.

For example, the system could comprise multiple independent threads of computation, each performing some subtask of a larger optimization problem, such as running a family of simulations, designing a series of components, carrying out an empirical investigation, or solving a mathematical problem. Each such thread could in itself be highly intelligent, possibly even generally intelligent. But no thread would have to last for very long. Sometimes a single thread might spawn several others, while at other times multiple threads might merge, combining their results. No single thread of computation, nor any set of threads, would constitute an individual, analogous to a human being, with a life of its own. Issues that plague humans, such as that of personal survival, simply would not arise for such an AI or for any of its parts.

What would it be like to interact with such an AI? With more direct means at their disposal for the transmission of information, the multiple intelligent threads within the system wouldn't need to use human-like language to communicate with each other or to coordinate their activities. But this doesn't imply that the system would be unable to use language to communicate with humans. A good model of human behavior, the sort of model a superintelligent AI would be able to construct, would necessarily incorporate a model of the way humans use language. The AI would be adept at exploiting such a model, deploying words and sentences to gather information from humans, to impart information to humans, and to influence human behavior in order to realize its goals and maximize its expected reward.

The mechanisms for dealing with language that this sort of engineered superintelligence would use seem so different from those found in the human brain that it's questionable whether it could be said to *understand* language at all.[2] When humans speak to each other, there is the shared assumption of mutual empathy. You understand me when I say I am sad because you have experienced sadness yourself, and I have an expectation that your actions, whether sympathetic or harsh, are at least informed by this understanding. This assumption would be unwarranted for an AI based on a sophisticated combination of optimization and machine learning algorithms. Such an AI would be perfectly capable of using emotive language in imitation of humans. But it wouldn't do so out of empathy. Nor would it be out of deceptive malice. It would be for purely instrumental reasons.

The upshot would be a powerful illusion when talking to the AI. We might call it the illusion that "someone is at home." It would seem as if we were interacting with something—with someone—like us, someone whose behavior is to some extent predictable because they are like us. To make the illusion complete, the AI could use an *avatar*, a robot body that it temporarily inhabits in order to participate directly in the world and on the same apparent terms as humans. (Indeed the AI could inhabit multiple avatars simultaneously.) This would be a handy trick in many ways. But above all, it would expedite linguistic behavior, enabling the AI to use facial cues, body language, and so on, as well as to engage in cooperative physical activities with humans.

In computer science, the *user illusion* is the feeling that we are interacting with real objects when, for example, we use a mouse to move folders around on a desktop. Creating such an illusion facilitates human–computer interaction. But no one thinks they are manipulating actual physical objects, real folders on a real desktop. In the study of animal behavior, *anthropomorphism* is the unwarranted attribution of human-like thoughts to nonhuman animals, such as when I assert that Tooty (the family cat) ignores us because we are merely his servants. With artificial intelligence, especially the sort of superintelligent AI envisaged here, it's all too easy for the user illusion, a good thing, to shade over into anthropomorphism, which is bad.

Why would this be bad? After all, if the illusion were sufficiently complete, what would it matter that the effect was generated by a mechanism with no resemblance to the biological brain? Perhaps anthropomorphism isn't the problem here. Perhaps the allegation of anthropomorphism is itself a symptom of *biocentrism*, an irrational prejudice against intelligence of a nonbiological character. Well, the worry is that after days, weeks, or years of normal, human-like interaction with the AI, we would misguidedly come to expect its behavior to continue in the same comprehensible vein indefinitely. If the user illusion were convincing enough, we would forget about the fundamentally alien character of the AI. We would forget that an AI of this kind uses language for purely instrumental purposes, to help maximize its future reward.

Imagine the following scenario. You have worked for several years for a large corporation that is run by an AI. You are an excellent employee. You always beat your deadlines and exceed your targets, and have been steadily moving up the company hierarchy. A couple of years ago you had some family difficulties, and had to negotiate some time off and a salary increase to cope. Your negotiations, all in natural language and by voice, were exclusively with the AI. No humans were involved. But the AI seemed to listen sympathetically, seemed to understand your troubles. It offered sound personal advice, and agreed to everything you asked. Then one day, without the slightest warning, without a hint of explanation, you are informed that you're fired.

Of course, this kind of thing happens often enough with human bosses. But it's safe to assume that a human boss, however nasty, can put himself in your shoes. He can imagine what it's like to receive such a blow, even if he seems indifferent (perhaps even to revel in your discomfort). With a human boss, you might appeal for a change of heart. You might paint a picture of your impoverished family and hope to stir pity, to elicit feelings of guilt. Your pleading might not work. But it would be worth a try. The sort of AI envisaged here, in contrast, would lack the affective substrate, the capacity for empathy, to make it even worth trying. You would have to accept that all the sympathy you got from the AI in the past was fake, just a pattern of sounds designed to elicit behavior from you that helped the AI to achieve its goals.

AI AND CONSCIOUSNESS

5.1 Would a Brain-Inspired AI Be Conscious?

The previous chapter mooted the idea of making and destroying copies of a simulated brain. This idea raises a philosophically difficult question, a question that leads to a host of concerns about the feasibility, not to say the wisdom, of creating brain-based human-level AIs. In particular, if a human-level AI were built that closely followed the organizational principles of the biological brain, would it not only act and think like its biological precursors, but also have feelings as they do? If it did, then how would it feel about the prospect of being copied, and of some of its copies eventually being destroyed?

More generally, what (if anything) would a brain-based AI feel about its "life," perhaps confined to virtual reality and obliged to work as a slave? If this sounds like a frivolous question, then recall that our current concern is with a form of artificial intelligence that is not only (at least) human-level, but also fundamentally human-like, thanks to its neural constitution. Shortly we'll consider the question of consciousness in other forms of AI, engineered varieties for which such sensibilities may not be relevant. But for now our focus is on artifacts that work in a very similar way to the biological brain, albeit in emulation. Since they work in a similar way, they will think and behave in a similar way, so it makes sense to wonder whether or not they would feel in a similar way.

Some theorists have argued that metabolism—a continuous exchange of matter and energy with the environment that serves to maintain the boundary between self and other—is a prerequisite for consciousness.[1] According to this view, an artifact that lacked metabolism could not be credited with consciousness. This seems to rule out consciousness in any computer simulated brain, even a perfectly accurate whole brain emulation, although it still leaves room for a conscious AI built out of biological neurons, or that is based on synthetic biology. But other theorists favor functionalist views of consciousness that focus on the way a system (e.g., a brain) is organized rather than its material substrate.[2]

The issue can be put on a firmer footing with a thought experiment.[3] Consider again the mouse whole brain emulation discussed in chapter 2. There we imagined producing the emulation by scanning the mouse's brain, then producing a high-fidelity, neuron-for-neuron and synapse-for-synapse simulation based on the scan. But suppose instead that we produced an emulation by gradually replacing each neuron, one by one, in the living mouse with a functionally equivalent electronic surrogate. After the first neuron is replaced by its electronic counterpart and the biological original destroyed, the mouse's behavior should be unaffected. It will run away from cats, as before. It will still be attracted to cheese. It will recognize its kin and huddle with them just as it always did. The same should be true after the second, the third, the one-hundredth, and the one-millionth neuron are replaced, until eventually we end up with a mouse whose behavior is indistinguishable from that of the original even though its brain is 100 percent new and artificial.

We needn't concern ourselves here with the technological feasibility of this process, since here we are only conducting a thought experiment. As long as the process is theoretically possible, the thought experiment is valid. Now, most people would agree that a mouse—a normal biological mouse—enjoys a degree of *consciousness*. A mouse, we assume, can experience hunger and pain. It is aware of its surroundings—scents and textures, sights, and sounds. These are all aspects of consciousness. The question is what happens to the mouse's consciousness in our thought experiment. What happens to its capacity for suffering, for example, as its neurons are gradually replaced, one by one? (We will assume the process itself is painless, of course.)

Is there, perhaps, a point at which the mouse's consciousness *suddenly disappears*? After the replacement of neuron 239,457 perhaps? This doesn't seem very plausible. So perhaps its consciousness *gradually fades*. Outwardly, the mouse seems the same throughout the procedure. It continues to seek out cheese, to squeal when subjected to electric shock, and so on. But the "hunger itself," the inner feeling, slowly disappears, even though to an outside observer nothing has changed. On this view, there is something mysteriously important about the biology of real neurons. Their biological character somehow generates a nimbus of consciousness, something that has no connection with behavior—what philosophers call an "epiphenomenon."

Then again, perhaps the mouse's consciousness *persists throughout* the procedure. Perhaps it not only can feel pain before any of its neurons are replaced but also can feel pain when half of them have been exchanged for digital equivalents, and still can feel pain when the whole lot have been exchanged and its brain is fully electronic. On this view, nothing changes outwardly, and nothing changes inwardly either. This possibility seems at least as plausible as the gradual fading alternative.

Is there an argument that favors one of these possibilities over the other? Well, let's move up from the mouse brain and consider the human case. It's easier to believe the neuronal replacement procedure would work with a small mouse brain. But the thought experiment can be extended to a brain of any size. Once again, we should suppose that the behavior of our human subject is unaffected. Outwardly—even to her closest family and friends—she seems the same person, even as more and more of her neurons are replaced by electronic equivalents. She still listens to the same music, tells the same stories about her college days, and so on. Moreover, when questioned, she maintains that she feels nothing unusual. Yes, she insists, of course she is still conscious. She is aware of the color of the sky, of the wind brushing her face. All this follows from the premise of the thought experiment—that behavior is the outcome of physical processes that can be replicated *in silico*.

But by the time all her neurons have been substituted for artificial surrogates, should we still believe these pronouncements? Or should we be skeptical? Perhaps she has turned into a "zombie," in the philosophers' sense, a creature that behaves like a real person despite that fact that it has no inner life. There is, so to speak, no one at home. If this seems a likely outcome, consider the following extension of the thought experiment. Suppose the replacement process is now *reversed*. One by one, our subject's electronic neurons are replaced by genuine biological equivalents until she is, once again, a wholly organic being. Even according to the gradual fading hypothesis, she should then be back to normal, her consciousness properly restored.

Now, suppose she is interviewed at various times during the procedure, and asked about her state of mind. What would she say? Would she, at some point, announce with relief that her consciousness was returning, that she had been "sort of absent" (or some such thing), but that she was feeling fine now? No—this is ruled out by the premise of the thought experiment. The subject's outward behavior would be the same as if her neurons were untouched. She will continue to assert that her consciousness is unimpaired. Moreover she will unwaveringly claim to remember conscious experiences from all the earlier stages of the experiment, including the stage when her brain was 100 percent artificial. Indeed, if you (human reader) were the subject of this experiment, you would be similarly insistent.

So are we to doubt her, to assume these memories of conscious awareness are illusory? Would you doubt your own memory of the wind in your face as you walked to work this morning if it were suddenly revealed to you that all the neurons in your brain were, at that time, artificial replacements? Would you be convinced by a philosopher who argued that the earlier you was in fact a mere zombie, experiencing nothing but behaving just like you while false memories of conscious experience were simultaneously being implanted? If not, then you are a type of *functionalist*.

You favor the notion that consciousness persists throughout the procedure, that what counts is a neuron's function rather than its biological constitution.

It should be clear that, at those times in the thought experiment when the participants are all digital, they are (almost) equivalent to whole brain emulations. They differ only in their bodies. The thought experiment participants retain biological bodies, whereas the kinds of whole brain emulation we have so far envisaged either have artificial (nonbiological) robot bodies or exist in virtual reality and have virtual bodies. Are there any implications for the functionalist of these different forms of embodiment? In particular, could it be the case that only the *biologically* embodied artificial brain would be conscious? Or perhaps it is *physical* embodiment that matters but not the particular type of physical embodiment, in which case the biologically embodied artificial brain and the brain with the artificial robot body would both be conscious but the virtually embodied artificial brain would not.

All these philosophical positions are perfectly reasonable. However, let's stick with the most liberal brand of functionalism for now, and see how far we can push it. Let's suppose that each of these whole brain emulations, however it is embodied, deserves to be called conscious just as much as the fully biological original. But whole brain emulation is at the extreme end of a spectrum of biological fidelity. What about consciousness in a designer brain?

What about an artificial intelligence whose construction broadly follows the organizational principles of the biological brain but doesn't match the brain of any actual biological species, let alone that of any individual specimen? How far could we depart from the biological blueprint without undermining the conditions that allow consciousness to arise?

What we really need in order to answer this question is an established general scientific theory of consciousness, one that encompasses all the forms that consciousness might take. A sufficiently broad theory should answer the question not only for biologically inspired artificial intelligence but also for AI that has been engineered from scratch, for intelligent artifacts that differ from the biological brain at their most fundamental level of operation. In the context of superintelligent AI, perhaps it even makes sense to speak of different kinds of consciousness, or of levels of consciousness that go beyond the human. A properly mature theory might cover this possibility too. Unfortunately though, no such theory has yet gained wide acceptance. Indeed there is no a clear consensus on what such a theory would even look like.

However, there are several viable candidates, such as Bernard Baars's *global workspace theory* and Giulio Tononi's theory of *integrated information*.[4] We won't go into these or any other theories of consciousness in any detail here.

However, it is worth noting something that these two leading contenders have in common. Both Baars's theory and Tononi's theory characterize consciousness as essentially a brain-wide, or system-wide phenomenon. When a person has a conscious experience, according to this way of thinking, they are in a state that implicates their whole brain, or a large portion of it. It involves their long- and short-term memory, their language center, their emotion, their imagination. It is not something that arises just in some localized part of the brain. It is a global, integrated, distributed, holistic property.

Holistic theories like these allow for consciousness in kinds of AI that are radically different from the biological brain because they are very liberal in their organizational requirements. Even with additional prerequisites for consciousness, such as embodied interaction with a complex environment, these theories allow for a vast range of conscious entities within the space of possible AIs. Moreover such theories typically marry the functional requirements of consciousness with organizational features that underlie sophisticated cognition: a holistic system (e.g., a brain) that supports global, integrated processes and states will be capable of bringing its fullest resources to bear on the ongoing situation. Although this doesn't entail that consciousness and general intelligence always go hand-in-hand, it does lend support to the idea that they coincide in brain-like architectures.

5.2 The Life of a Brain-Based AI

In the absence of an adequate theory, we cannot say with confidence how widespread consciousness is in the space of possible AIs. But there does seem to be a good case for consciousness in some portion of it. The question of whether or not an artificial intelligence would be conscious is an important one because it influences the range of morally acceptable options for future research. The 18th-century philosopher Jeremy Bentham asserted our moral duty toward other animals when he pointed out that the question is not "Can they reason?" or "Can they talk?" but "Can they suffer?" This is also the question to ask with respect to a human-level artificial intelligence. Could it suffer? If the answer is yes, then perhaps we should think twice before bringing it into the world, and if we do bring it into the world, then we are obliged to treat it well.[5]

Consider, for example, the prospect of a team of brain-based human-level AIs confined to virtual reality and forced to work as slaves, such as those in the motorbike design story. Suppose these AIs are prevented from doing anything else apart from work on problems set by their human owners and masters. Moreover, to maximize their effectiveness, they are ruthlessly parallelized. Multiple copies of each AI are made and set to work on variations of a problem or made to try out different avenues for solving it. After working for a while, the most promising copies are retained and the fruits of their labors assimilated into the work of the wider team. Those that are less successful are terminated.

If these were human workers, such conditions would be considered worse than brutal. The AIs have no life beyond work, and they are perpetually under the threat of death if they perform poorly. Of course, if the AIs are "mindless automata" who lack consciousness, and therefore lack the capacity to suffer, this doesn't matter. But suppose they are conscious. Suppose they experience their predicament just as a human would. To create such artifacts and subject them to this sort of existence would be morally reprehensible. Moreover, if they are at all human-like, they are likely to be uncooperative. An unhappy workforce is liable to go on strike, or to rebel. A truly unhappy workforce might want to start a revolution. If it comprised superintelligent AIs, it would more than likely be successful, to the detriment of humanity.

We have been considering the prospect of a virtually embodied brain-based artificial intelligence. Do similar considerations apply if the putative AI is physically embodied, that is to say a robot? Well, the reasons for endowing a robot with human-level intelligence would perhaps not be the same as the motivation for building a virtually embodied human-level AI. In both cases we are assuming that embodiment is so central to cognition in the biological brain that it couldn't be dispensed with in a brain-based AI. (Shortly we'll revisit AI engineered from scratch, where a whole other set of issues arises.) But a physically embodied AI couldn't be accelerated to work at biologically unrealistic speeds. Nor would it be so easy to make multiple copies of a physically embodied AI in order to exploit parallelism. So, rather than being a stepping stone to superintelligence, robots might be endowed with human-level AI to enable them to do things that humans do today—to work in factories, say, or to do manual labor, or perhaps to provide a form of companionship.

Then again, the distinction between virtual and physical embodiment would become less relevant if an AI could easily migrate between virtual reality and physical reality (much like the characters in the *Matrix* triology), taking on a robot body as an avatar in order to interact with the physical world. This would be one way in which a disaffected and rebelious AI (or indeed a malicious or malfunctioning AI) could escape the confines of virtual reality and wreak havoc in the real world. But there are other ways that require nothing more than Internet access. Consider Stuxnet, the weaponized computer virus that infiltrated computers in an Iranian nuclear facility, where it took control of centrifuges that were being used to enrich uranium.

We'll look more closely at the various risks associated with sophisticated AI technology in due course. For now though, the issue is a narrow one. Would it make moral and practical sense to build human- or superhuman-level artificial intelligences that conformed to the blueprint of the biological brain, given that humans are conscious creatures with complex emotional lives? From a moral standpoint, if such an AI were capable of suffering, its creators would be ethically obliged to ensure its well-being. Even from the standpoint of someone who is skeptical about artificial consciousness, there are practical reasons to exercise caution. Failing to ensure the "well-being" of a team of human-like "zombie" AIs would lead to an unproductive workforce, since even a zombie AI would behave *as if* it had feelings.

How might the developer of human-like AI circumvent these difficulties? Since the manufacturers of the AI could offer access to its brain's reward system, one option would be to adopt the methods of a tyrant. The owner of a team of AIs could submit them to the harshest possible conditions in order to maximize their productivity and directly stimulate their pain centers if they resisted. But even for the skeptic who insists that the resulting pain behavior is fake, that an artificial brain can only have simulated pain, this would be a risky strategy, especially if the AIs in question had superhuman intelligence. If such an AI escaped and decided to exact revenge, it would not be especially comforting to know that the AI was only motivated by "fake" anger.

A more palatable strategy would be to provide the very best living conditions for the AIs, and to reward them for doing their jobs well. As with a human workforce, this policy is likely to be most productive in the long run, is less dangerous, and raises fewer ethical issues. Taking this liberal approach to its limit, we can imagine a sufficiently human-like AI being given the same legal status and the same rights as a human. At the same time it would acquire moral responsibilities and would be subject to the law like any person. Perhaps the eventual result would be a society in which biological and artificial intelligence coexisted harmoniously, as envisaged in the *Culture* novels of Iain Banks.

This vision of the future has considerable appeal. If the transition from human-level AI to superintelligence is inevitable, then it would be a good idea to ensure that artificial intelligence inherits basic human motives and values. These might include intellectual curiosity, the drive to create, to explore, to improve, to progress. But perhaps the value we should inculcate in AI above all others is compassion toward others, toward all sentient beings, as Buddhists say. And despite humanity's failings—our war-like inclinations, our tendency to perpetuate inequality, and our occasional capacity for cruelty—these values do seem to come to the fore in times of abundance. So the more human-like an AI is, the more likely it will be to embody the same values, and the more likely it is that humanity will move toward a utopian future, one in which we are valued and afforded respect, rather than a dystopian future in which we are treated as worthless inferiors.

With that thought in mind, perhaps we should be wary of a third way to prevent the creation of a disaffected brain-based AI, namely to fundamentally re-engineer the brain's reward system. Our discussion of this issue has so far assumed an AI whose brain adheres closely to the vertebrate blueprint—something that starts out as a generic, neonatal, or infantile vertebrate brain with the capacity to attain human-level intelligence and beyond through development and learning. But what if the reward system of such a brain were re-designed so that its only motivation was to serve humanity? At the same time its capacity to feel anything negative such as pain, hunger, tiredness, or frustration could be removed. Indeed any emotions that were considered superfluous from an engineering standpoint could be eliminated. Sexuality could be dispensed with, for example, along with the desire to nurture children. Wouldn't the result be the ideal servant, the perfect slave?

It is by no means obvious that general intelligence is attainable in an emotionally eviscerated brain-based AI. In humans, emotion is intimately bound up with decision making and integral to creativity. Moreover, as remarked in the previous chapter, one hallmark of human intelligence is our ability to transcend the reward function we have inherited from biology through reason and reflection. But in order to succeed in rendering their product safe, neural engineers would not only have to redesign the brain's motivational system, they would also have to fix the resulting reward function permanently to prevent it from being subsumed by something less predictable and more dangerous.

At the same time they would perhaps limit what even a superintelligent AI could accomplish outside of the sphere of science and technology.

If human-level artificial intelligence is developed by taking inspiration from the biological brain, then the way ethical and pragmatic issues like these are tackled will dramatically influence our future as a species. If, instead, human-level artificial intelligence is engineered from scratch, a different set of considerations apply. But their implications are equally weighty. The very prospect of machines with human-level intelligence and beyond obliges us to ask the most fundamental questions. What sort of world do we want to create, to bequeath to our future selves, our descendants, or our successors? Do we want the AIs of the future to be our servants and slaves, or to be our companions and equals, or to supplant us in evolutionary terms? A greater understanding of the spectrum of possible AIs will better position us to steer the future in the direction we want it to go. Or if the trajectory of technology is predetermined, the inevitable result of unstoppable economic, social, and political forces, it will help us be prepared.

5.3 Consciousness in Engineered Superintelligence

As we have seen, it's reasonable to expect a brain-based human-level AI to be fairly human-like, and to attribute to it something like the sort of conscious inner life we biological humans enjoy. A brain-based superintelligence might be harder to comprehend than a plain old human-level AI, but there is no reason to expect a higher level of intelligence to abolish this inner life. On the contrary, we might expect the conscious inner life of such an AI to be especially rich. But what about a superintelligent AI that was engineered from scratch? If its inner workings were nothing like those of the brain, to what extent, if any, would it be appropriate to call such an AI conscious? This is an important question, not only because it informs how we should treat such artifacts—whether we have the right to damage, disable, or destroy them—but also because it informs how we should expect them to treat us.

Recall the nasty AI boss, for example. How likely is it that machine superintelligence (if it arises) will conform to the disturbing portrait of a heartless machine pursuing its own ends by tricking us into thinking it cares? Could it turn out that such an AI would somehow develop the basis for empathy, or that the basis for empathy could be designed into it? Why do consciousness and empathy matter anyway? Couldn't a superintelligent AI lack these things yet still act in a perfectly comprehensible and benign way? We have touched on the topic of consciousness a few times already. But this thicket of questions brings us to the edge of some particularly difficult philosophical territory. To navigate it, we need to make some careful distinctions.

Referring to the challenge of explaining consciousness in scientific terms, the philosopher David Chalmers distinguishes between what he calls the "hard problem" and the "easy problem."[6] The so-called easy problem of consciousness (which isn't easy at all) is the challenge of elucidating the mechanisms that underpin the cognitive capacities we associate with consciousness, such as a person's ability to understand their situation by integrating information from their senses, or to describe in words how they are feeling and what they are thinking, or to recall events from their past. Notably, these cognitive capacities have behavioral manifestations. They help us get around in the world, to maintain our well-being, to achieve our goals and to be part of society.

The "hard problem" of consciousness, however, is the challenge of explaining in scientific terms why it is *like something* to be a conscious creature (to use the terminology of another philosopher, Thomas Nagel).[7] How is it that we have subjective sensations and feelings? How is it that this subjective visual experience I am having right now, the blur of English countryside flying past the train window, can arise in my brain? The difficulty here stems from the skeptical thought that arises when I look at my fellow passengers. Whatever their behavior, whatever they do or say—even if they stare wistfully at the view and comment on its beauty—it seems at least logically possible that they are actually experiencing nothing. I have no access to their private, inner world, so how can I be certain that they even have one? Perhaps they are just zombies, just automata.

The philosophical effect of this skeptical thought is not really to instill doubt but rather to draw attention to an apparent division between two aspects of consciousness—an outer aspect, which has an objective behavioral manifestation, and an inner aspect, which is purely subjective and private. Some philosophers believe that explaining the inner aspect in scientific terms—the hard problem—is impossible. Nevertheless, many of the same philosophers will grant that the easy problem is soluble, that the outer aspect of consciousness can be scientifically explained, by elucidating the mechanisms that give rise to the associated collection of cognitive capacities.

Now, what does any of this have to do with AI? Well, we need to be clear about the inner/outer distinction to prevent us from getting in a muddle when we discuss the different implications of various sorts of AI. If our concern is whether we have a moral duty toward the artifacts we have created, then what matters is whether they have consciousness in the inner sense, whether it is like something to be the AI. But if our concern is the impact the AI will have on human society, then we can confine our discussion to the outer aspect of consciousness. As far as having a positive impact on humanity is concerned, it makes no difference whether a superintelligent machine is "really" conscious—conscious on the inside, so to speak—whether it "really" feels empathy toward us. It is enough for it to behave *as if* it were conscious. If it behaves *as if* it felt empathy toward us, then that's good enough.

But it does matter that an AI that merely behaves *as if* it feels empathy continues to do so indefinitely. We don't want the AI, after affecting empathy for a while, to unexpectedly turn on us. So how can we ensure that this doesn't happen? One approach is to make the AI very human-like, and one way to do this is to make its architecture very brain-like. The more closely an AI conforms to the biological blueprint, the more confident we can be that its actions will forever reflect the fundamental system of values we impart to it, even if its intelligence is enhanced. But our present focus is the kind of AI that has been engineered from scratch.

To understand how this sort of AI might behave, we need to prize apart the set of cognitive attributes associated with consciousness because, although they invariably go together in humans, in an AI they might arise separately. With these cognitive attributes duly prized apart, we'll be in a position to address the following question, which in turn will take us back to the thicket of questions at the start of this section. To what extent do general intelligence and consciousness (in its outer aspect) go hand in hand everywhere in the space of possible AIs? Perhaps superintelligence can do without the full complement of cognitive attributes we associate with human consciousness.

But maybe some subset of them is required, entailing that a superintelligent AI will necessarily possess a kind of consciousness, albeit of an alien sort.

Three cognitive attributes that seem to be not only necessary for consciousness but also intimately tied together are (1) an apparent sense of purpose, (2) an awareness of the world and the ongoing situation, and (3) the ability to integrate knowledge, perception, and action. When we see one animal chase another (e.g., a cat and a mouse), we immediately ascribe a sense of *purpose* to them both. One animal wants to catch the other. The other animal wants to escape. These aims take their place in a complex set of goals and needs that we assume animals to have, enabling us to make sense of and predict their behavior. In short, we see their behavior as purposeful. An animal manifests an *awareness* of its surroundings when it perceives the ongoing situation and responds to it in a way that is consistent with its goals and needs, as the mouse does when it spies a hole and disappears into it to escape.

Finally, an animal exhibits full cognitive *integration* when its actions cohere not only with what it perceives of the ongoing situation, but also with what it has perceived in the past and with what it has come to know as a consequence. The cat, for instance, knows that the mouse is down there somewhere, that it's worth waiting by the hole in case it re-appears, and also that it can pester its owner if food (rather than fun) is what it really wants. The contrast here with, say, my 2015 laptop is huge. It is impossible to see my laptop as exhibiting purposeful behavior or having any kind of autonomy. In no meaningful sense is it aware of its environment, even if we interpret that term generously to include, say, the Internet. It isn't capable of usefully integrating the information it holds or has access to in order to better attain its goals or meet its needs, since it doesn't really have any.

However, it doesn't take much to endow an artifact with rudimentary versions of these three attributes. Robot vacuum cleaners and self-driving cars both exhibit a degree of awareness of their environment, and are able to respond to ongoing events in a way that coheres with their simple goals. Disembodied personal assistants don't give the same impression of autonomy or purpose. But they can integrate information of various kinds from different sources, including browsing habits, GPS data, calendar entries, and so on. With the increasing convergence and sophistication of these technologies, the illusion of a mind-like entity behind the screen and voice will become more complete.

Now, what of a superintelligent AI? It's difficult to see how a system could possess general intelligence, let alone superintelligence, unless it displayed these three cognitive attributes. Unlike a robot vacuum cleaner, whose goals are so simple that we fully understand them after a few minutes of observation, the overarching motives behind the behavior of a superintelligent AI might be hard to fathom. Yet it would surely have to pursue various subsidiary goals, goals that a human could more easily comprehend, and this would leave us in no doubt that its behavior was purposeful. Moreover, to warrant the ascription of general intelligence, the AI would certainly have to maintain an awareness of the world it inhabited (whether real or virtual), and to respond to ongoing events in a way that manifests this awareness.

Finally, we would expect an artificial superintelligence to display a high degree of cognitive integration. It should be able to bring its full battery of cognitive resources to bear on whatever problem it is trying to solve, combining everything it has learned through its endowment of sensors and data feeds. Taken together, these three cognitive attributes—purpose, awareness, and integration—would give any human who interacted with or observed such an artificial intelligence the impression of a single, unified, intellect of great power. In short, according to this argument, a superintelligent AI would necessarily exhibit the outward traits of a kind of consciousness.

5.4 Self-Awareness in Superintelligence

Now let's turn to some other attributes that, in humans, we associate with consciousness, beginning with *self-awareness*. In the second movie of the *Terminator* franchise, the trouble starts when the fictional AI system Skynet "becomes self-aware." But what does self-awareness mean for humans, and what might it mean for a real AI? Is it necessary for artificial general intelligence? Or is it an optional characteristic, which would open up the possibility of a superintelligent AI that manifests a very alien kind of consciousness? Once again, our concern here is with the outward manifestations of this cognitive attribute, and we can set aside the philosophically difficult issue of subjectivity, of what it's like to be self-aware, what it is like on the inside, so to speak.

For humans (and other animals), there is a fairly well-defined lump of matter with a clear location in space that is an obvious focus for self-awareness in this outward, cognitively relevant sense, namely the body. We are aware of the configuration of our limbs, of internal bodily states such as hunger or tiredness. But human self-awareness isn't only about the body. Even when viewed strictly as a cognitive attribute with behavioral implications, human self-awareness pertains to the mind as well as the body. Humans are aware of their own beliefs, of their own plans, of their own unfolding thoughts and emotions. This is not to say that the beliefs we form about our own beliefs, goals, and thoughts are always on the mark. But we have some access to these things, and are capable of usefully reflecting on them. Not only do I not know the time of the next train to London, I know that I don't know, and can plan to remedy this by consulting a timetable.

I am also aware of an ongoing sequence of thoughts and feelings that belongs to me, my "stream of consciousness" as William James called it.[8] I know that this stream of consciousness stops when I am asleep (and not dreaming). Poignantly, I can reflect on the ultimate fate, not only of my physical body but also of my stream of consciousness, and I can take steps to prolong my life so as to postpone this fate as long as possible. In these various senses I am aware of my own existence and have an instinct to protect this existence, for self-preservation.

Now, to what extent is self-awareness in any of these senses necessary for an AI with human- or superhuman-level intelligence? On the one hand, like the three other cognitive attributes we have just looked at, it's difficult to imagine how anything could be called generally intelligent if it were incapable of reflecting on its own beliefs, its own plans, and its own reasoning processes. No superintelligence worth its salt would allow its avatar to end up sitting on a bench having just missed the train to London. Neither, more seriously, would we expect it to miss the opportunity to optimize its reasoning processes by noting which problem-solving strategies have been successful in the past.

On the other hand, there are certain aspects of human self-awareness that are less applicable to artificial intelligence. For instance, it may or may not be the case that an AI is embodied. Of course, if an AI is embodied, or if it deploys an avatar, then the behavior of the robotic body in question must exhibit a sensitivity to the configuration of its bodily parts. Otherwise, it would fall over or crash or drop things. But because we can envisage a disembodied superintelligent AI, this aspect of self-awareness isn't a necessary accompaniment to general intelligence. More tricky, though, is the question of an AI's awareness of its very existence, and the potential drive for self-preservation this seems to entail. Is this aspect of self-awareness, so important for humans, a necessary accompaniment of artificial general intelligence?

The issue here is what constitutes the identity of an AI. What, exactly, would be the thing of whose existence it might be aware, that it would seek to preserve? What, indeed, is the "it" in all these sentences? Once again we are approaching philosophically difficult territory. The question of personal identity is one that both Western and Eastern philosophies have wrestled with for millennia. But, to reiterate, our concern here is strictly with functional and behavioral issues. The kind of AI that's under discussion is not engineered to be a philosopher but to maximize expected reward over time. Moreover the task here is to imagine the space of possible AIs of this sort. In this context, what we want to know is which aspects of self-awareness, if any, are necessary for general intelligence. Being clear about which

Is this aspect of self-awareness, so important for humans, a necessary accompaniment of artificial general intelligence?

aspects are *not* necessary will ensure that we don't make false anthropomorphic assumptions about the nature of machine superintelligence.

As already noted, we can imagine a disembodied AI, so there is no reason to expect a superintelligent AI to identify itself with a particular physical body with arms, legs, tentacles, and so on. Moreover it wouldn't make sense for an AI to identify itself with a specific collection of computer hardware, since the same code can be executed in a distributed fashion over many separate processors and can migrate from one platform to another without its execution even being interrupted. Nor, for similar reasons, would the AI identify itself with a particular codebase. Software is mutable. It can be debugged, upgraded, extended, or re-designed, perhaps even by the AI itself. (Recall too the prospect of a system comprising multiple, semiautonomous threads of intelligent computation, each having just a fleeting existence.)

What other candidates are there for what might constitute the self of an AI? Though conceivable, it would be peculiar if an AI identified itself as the nonphysical subject of a series of thoughts and experiences floating free of the physical world. Science fiction films often invoke such notions. But there is no guarantee that a superintelligent AI would have this sort of inner life. Even if it did, this idea of selfhood rests on a dualistic conception of reality that is of dubious applicability to humans, let alone to artificial intelligence. There is no particular reason to expect a superintelligent AI to adopt a metaphysical stance of such doubtful standing, especially—and here is an important point—if it has no bearing on its ability to maximize expected reward.[9]

What about self-preservation? As far as self-preservation is concerned, it does seem plausible that the powerful optimizer at the heart of a superintelligent AI would seek to preserve its own reward function, along with the means to maximize that reward function over time. As well as certain computer processes (and sufficient hardware to execute them), the means to maximize reward could encompass resources such as the data those processes have access to, including real-time information from sensors, plus the effectors and other equipment those processes can control (e.g., satellites or military hardware) and the various capacities and powers they can exercise (e.g., the ability to trade stocks or to enter into contracts with other parties).

However, the preservation of these things would be a purely instrumental aim, subserving the overarching drive to maximize reward over time. It might be the case that the set of computer processes the optimizer sought to preserve would include those constituting the optimizer itself, giving the appearance of self-awareness. But it might not. It should be borne in mind that reward is not *for* the AI. It is just a function that the AI seeks to maximize. The AI doesn't even need to be around to "receive" it. If the AI's reward function involves maximizing widget production, then the optimal strategy might be to commission a widget factory and then self-destruct (like the proverbial sea squirt who finds a rock to stick to then digests its own brain).

5.5 Emotion and Empathy in Superintelligence

Let's take a moment to recap. We have been looking into various cognitive attributes that are associated with consciousness in humans, and asking whether or not we should expect to see them in a human- or superhuman-level AI. The sort of AI we're focusing on now does not resemble the human brain. It has been engineered from scratch. So it's possible that it is not very human-like, that it manifests none of the traits we associate with consciousness in humans. Nevertheless, some of those cognitive attributes seem to be an inevitable accompaniment of general intelligence. In particular, awareness, purpose, and integration are all likely to feature in any artificial general intelligence, giving the impression of a certain sort of consciousness. Then again, self-awareness, another important feature of human consciousness, though likely to be present in an AI, may take on a rather unfamiliar form.

The final attributes associated with human consciousness that we're going to examine are emotion and empathy.

From a purely cognitive standpoint, the machine learning component of an artificial general intelligence is bound to notice the statistical regularities in human behavior that correlate with states we label as emotional. Not to pick up on these regularities would be to miss an opportunity to usefully compress human behavioral data into a mathematical model that can be used effectively to predict human behavior. Such a mathematical model would in turn be able to inform the optimization component of the AI, enabling it to manipulate human emotions, and in turn to modulate human behavior. In short, we should expect a superintelligent machine to know us better than we know ourselves.

It would also be a useful skill for an AI to be able to mimic emotion. Facial expressions and body language are a useful channel of communication between humans, and would be a vital part of the behavioral repertoire of an AI embodied in human-like form or with a humanoid avatar. Similarly tone of voice is useful for conveying pleasure, disappointment, anger, surprise, and so on. There is no need to fool people into thinking there are real emotions behind these cues. They function as communication aids regardless.

Still, as we saw with the story of the nasty AI boss, an AI that could convince people that it experienced real emotions would, under certain circumstances, be in a good position to maximize its reward function. It would be especially useful to be able to give the impression of empathy. Someone who feels sorry for us when we suffer will be disinclined to do us harm, and is therefore deserving of our trust. Similarly, if an AI appears to feel for us, then we will be inclined to trust it and to let it act autonomously. Of course, a superintelligent machine that knows us better than we know ourselves will be supremely capable of giving the impression of empathy.

Does this entail that a superintelligent AI is bound to pursue some wicked goal (e.g., world domination) with Machiavellian brilliance, effortlessly manipulating gullible humans and leading inevitably to our downfall? Not at all. The important question here might seem to be whether the AI *really* feels sorry for us or not, whether it is *truly* capable of empathy, because an AI that really felt for us would never do us harm while an AI that only imitates empathy is a dangerous psychopath. But what actually matters is not how the AI feels, but how it behaves. What actually matters is whether, like a true friend, it continues to act in the way we would like it to in the long run.

In the end, everything depends on the AI's reward function. From a cognitive standpoint, human-like emotions are a crude mechanism for modulating behavior. Unlike other cognitive attributes we associate with consciousness, there seems to be no logical necessity for an artificial general intelligence to behave as if it had empathy or emotion. If its reward function is suitably designed,

However, it is extremely difficult to design a reward function that is guaranteed not to produce undesirable behavior.

then its benevolence is assured. However, it is extremely difficult to design a reward function that is guaranteed not to produce undesirable behavior. As we'll see shortly, a flaw in the reward function of a superintelligent AI could be catastrophic. Indeed such a flaw could mean the difference between a utopian future of cosmic expansion and unending plenty, and a dystopian future of endless horror, perhaps even extinction.

THE IMPACT OF AI

6.1 The Politics and Economics of Human-Level AI

We have heard a number of arguments for the feasibility of human-level artificial intelligence, either via the brain-inspired route or through engineering from scratch. We saw that, once human-level AI is achieved, the genie could be out of the bottle. The transition from human-level AI to superintelligence seems inevitable, and could be very rapid. If there is an intelligence explosion, thanks to recursive self-improvement, then the resulting system or systems are likely to be very powerful. How they behave, whether they will be friendly or hostile, whether they will be predictable or inscrutable, whether conscious, capable of empathy or suffering, all depend on their underlying architecture and organization and the reward function they implicitly or explicitly implement.

It's hard to gauge which, if any, of the various kinds of AI that we can envisage today will actually arise. Nevertheless, we can try to think through some of the possible consequences for human society if machine superintelligence, in one form or another, becomes a reality. First, though, let's examine some of the economic, social, and political forces that might drive or arrest its development. Why would anyone want to create human-level artificial general intelligence in the first place? The most obvious motive is economic, and a primary focus for growth is *automation*. Of course, increasing automation has been the trend in industry since the 18th century. But many occupations that have traditionally been immune from this trend will be amenable to automation if artificial general intelligence is developed.

The occupations in question are those that are *AI-complete*. A problem is said to be AI-complete if achieving human-level AI is a prerequisite for building a computer that can solve it. Passing the Turing Test (properly) is an AI-complete problem, as is (professional standard) machine translation. Occupations such as lawyer, company executive, market researcher, scientist, programmer, psychiatrist, and many more, all appear to be AI-complete. To do them competently requires a commonsense understanding of the physical world and of human affairs, as well as a degree of creativity. But if human-level AI is achieved, then it will become feasible for machines to carry out such jobs, and to do so more cheaply and more effectively than humans (as long as they can be treated as slaves with moral impunity). So there will be a powerful economic incentive for corporations to develop the required technology.

Automation is just one potential growth area for sophisticated, general-purpose artificial intelligence. New technologies can engender whole new domains of application and lead to entirely redefined lifestyles. Consider the impact of the Internet or the smartphone. Artificial general intelligence has at least as much potential to infuse our daily lives. The indispensable household robot is a staple of science fiction. But the reality is more likely to be an ambient artificial intelligence that can temporarily "inhabit" a number of robot-like bodies such as cars, vacuum cleaners, and lawnmowers, as well as accompanying users in wearable or portable devices, and controlling any number of stationary household and workplace appliances such as cookers and 3D printers.

When you leave the house, the same conversation you were having with your vacuum cleaner or robot pet will be carried on seamlessly with your driverless car, as if one "person" inhabited all these devices. (Yet the underlying computations are likely to be distributed across multiple platforms that could be located anywhere in the world.) Though it won't appeal to everyone, this is an alluring picture. The promise of a huge market for AI-facilitated lifestyles is likely to drive the development of numerous enabling technologies, including computer vision, machine learning, natural language processing, and optimization.

Accumulated incremental improvements in these enabling technologies, along with the increasing use of pervasive sensing and the availability of ever-larger quantities of useful data on the Internet, might be enough to bring us to the edge of human-level AI. It might not require a major project or a conceptual breakthrough, just a clever but simple final step that enables the incorporation of creativity or some other missing ingredient. But, if a larger push is needed, the growing economic importance of special-purpose (i.e., nongeneral) AI technology is likely to ensure that funding and resources are available for relevant fundamental research.

The market economy is one factor in the drive toward artificial general intelligence. But there are ample reasons for state funding to accelerate its development too, reasons in addition to spurring economic growth. Military commanders might understandably have reservations over their roles being usurped by artificial intelligence. Nevertheless, the advent of *autonomous weapons* is creating the need for rapid decision making. For example, one rationale for using autonomous aerial vehicles for combat is speed and maneuverability. An autonomous aircraft can potentially detect, avoid, and neutralize a threat more quickly and accurately than any human pilot. Under these circumstances a human in the loop would slow things down.

If we factor in the likelihood that aerial combat will involve swarms of such aircraft pitted against each other, then the advantage of deploying AI to make rapid tactical decisions is obvious. Against this backdrop, the qualms of military commanders might vanish, motivating the acquisition of sophisticated AI technology for use at multiple levels of military decision making. The political dynamic here echoes the development of nuclear weapons in the 1940s and 1950s. At first, the chief motivation for developing a powerful weapon is the worry that the other side (whoever they are perceived to be) will get there first. This worry is enough to overcome any initial moral reservations. Then, when both sides have the weapon, an arms race ensues.

Despite this bleak assessment, the arguments in favor of the military use of AI are also worth attending to. Autonomous weapons are potentially more accurate and less error-prone than human combatants. They can be used more clinically, reducing so-called collateral damage. Their decisions are never influenced by fear, revenge, or anger. (Of course, we're not talking about human-like, brain-based AI here.) But our present focus is not the rights and wrongs of military AI. The point is simply that the potential for military application is another driving force for the future development of sophisticated AI technology.

Other motives for developing human-level AI are more idealistic. Centuries of technological progress have hugely benefited humankind. Thanks to advances in medicine and agriculture, hundreds of millions of people in the developed world enjoy a standard of living today that few could have dreamed of in the past, with comparatively excellent health care, nutrition, and longevity. We possess labor-saving devices that relieve the burden of daily chores such as cooking, washing, and cleaning. We have plentiful leisure time, and ways of enjoying it that would have seemed like magic to our ancestors. Nevertheless, humanity faces many global challenges, such as climate change, dwindling fossil fuels, ongoing conflicts, widespread poverty, and diseases that remain incurable like cancer and dementia.

The best hope for tackling these problems is surely through scientific and technological advances, and the best way to accelerate science and technology is surely to recruit, train, and apply more brilliant minds. So the arrival of human-level artificial intelligence, perhaps with a pattern of intellectual strengths and weaknesses that complements human intelligence, should lead to more rapid progress. If human-level AI is quickly succeeded by superhuman-level AI, perhaps precipitating an intelligence explosion, the rate of progress could be very fast indeed, provided that the resulting system behaves as we want it to. If optimistic commentators such as Ray Kurzweil are right, machine superintelligence could help bring about an era of unprecedented abundance in which poverty and disease are abolished.

But even this utopian vision looks pale alongside cosmological motives for developing machines with human-level intelligence and beyond. Roboticist Hans Moravec anticipates a far future in which a portion of the universe is "rapidly transformed into a cyberspace, [wherein beings] establish, extend, and defend identities as patterns of information flow ... becoming finally a bubble of Mind expanding at near lightspeed."[1] Unhampered by earthly biological needs, capable of withstanding extremes of temperature and doses of radiation that would be fatal to humans, and psychologically untroubled by the prospect of thousands of years traveling through interstellar space, self-reproducing superintelligent machines would be in a good position to colonize the galaxy. From a large enough perspective, it might be seen as human destiny to facilitate this future, even though (unenhanced) humans themselves are physically and intellectually too feeble to participate in it.

6.2 When Will Superintelligence Happen?

Some authors, notably Ray Kurzweil, have made very precise predictions about when machine superintelligence will arise. Writing in 2005, Kurzweil claimed that by the year 2045 the quantity of nonbiological intelligence on the planet will substantially exceed that of the entire human population.[2] He based his projections on *exponential technological trends*, extrapolating them into the future. The best known of these exponential trends is Moore's law, which we have already encountered several times. This states that the number of transistors that can be fabricated on a given area of silicon doubles roughly every eighteen months.

From the mid-1960s when it was proposed until the mid-2010s, the semiconductor industry managed to adhere to Moore's law, pulling a number of other computing statistics along with it. For example, the number of floating point operations per second (FLOPS) carried out by the world's fastest supercomputer has increased exponentially since the 1960s. Similar exponential trends are discernible in other areas of technology. In 1990 the human genome project set out to sequence the entire human genome in fifteen years. At the start of the project it was only possible to sequence 1 percent of the human genome per year. But DNA sequencing technology improved exponentially, and the project finished ahead of schedule in 2003, albeit at a cost of $2.7 billion. Little more than ten years later it became possible to sequence an individual's DNA for $1,000.

These and other exponential trends in technology exemplify what Kurzweil terms the *law of accelerating returns*. According to Kurzweil's theory, technological progress is governed by essentially the same principle as a financial investment with compound interest: the more you have, the faster it grows. If you invest x dollars in an account that yields 10 percent per annum, then after one year you have $1.1x$ dollars. But you earn more in the second year because your 10 percent is re-invested, yielding 10 percent of $1.1x$ dollars rather than 10 percent of just x dollars. Analogously, an area of technology is subject to the law of accelerating returns if improvements to that technology feed back into its development, thereby increasing the rate of improvement.

Kurzweil's 2045 date was obtained by (1) extrapolating the ongoing exponential increase in computing power per dollar and (2) estimating the amount of computing power that would be required to simulate the function of human cortex in real time. Kurzweil's extrapolated curve of exponentially increasing computing power hits 10^{26} instructions per second for $1,000 in the mid-2040s. Based on an estimate of 10^{16} instructions per second to simulate human cortex in real time, this would be enough for "the intelligence created per year [to be] about one billion times more powerful than all human intelligence [in the year 2005] ... representing a profound and disruptive transformation in human capability." This, for Kurzweil, is the singularity.

An obvious, but misguided, objection to Kurzweil's reasoning is that it seems to take for granted that Moore's law will continue into the 2040s. Indeed Moore's law is still more-or-less valid ten years on from Kurzweil's prediction.

But it has shown signs of slowing down, and is likely to plateau at some point in the 2020s. However, Moore's law is only part of a larger exponential trend. It describes one paradigm of computing technology, namely the large-scale integration of transistor circuitry on 2D wafers of silicon. In the 1960s, prior to the development of integrated circuits, computers were built out of individual transistors, and before that out of vacuum tubes. If the number of switching elements in a state-of-the-art machine is plotted against time, we obtain an exponential curve that stretches back to the mechanical devices of Pascal.

If we zoom in on this larger curve, we find that each distinct computing paradigm, from mechanical switches to large-scale integration, follows a pattern of initial slow growth while the technology is in its infancy, followed by rapid (exponential) growth, ending with a plateau when the technology reaches its fullest potential. The overall exponential, in other words, is made up of a series of smaller S-curves, one of which corresponds to Moore's law. The laws of physics ensure that the larger exponential trend will also reach a plateau eventually, and reveal itself to be just another, bigger S-curve. But there is a long way to go before that happens. (Recall Seth Lloyd's theoretically perfect computer.) In the meantime we should expect a succession of new computing paradigms to take over from the CMOS technology that has dominated the semiconductor industry for many decades.

A more potent criticism of Kurzweil's prediction is that it relies on the assumption that enough computing power will lead quickly to the development of human-level AI, and thus downplays the scientific progress that needs to be made to keep pace. Only the brute-force whole brain emulation approach can succeed simply by scaling up existing technology, and that depends on an exponential improvement in brain-scanning technology as well as computing power. Any other approach to human-level AI—whether through reverse engineering and re-engineering the biological brain or by engineering powerful algorithms from scratch—will require significant scientific breakthroughs.

There are grounds for optimism here. But these are insufficient to justify a confident prediction. For example, consider *C. elegans*. This tiny nematode worm is a model organism for biologists and has been the subject of countless studies. Its nervous system comprises just 302 neurons, and its full wiring diagram has been known since the 1980s. Nevertheless, a functional computer simulation of the *C. elegans* nervous system (and body) is still pending in the mid-2010s, although a crowdfunded open science project called OpenWorm is making good progress.[3] This, in large part, is due to a lack of fundamental data on the signaling properties of the 302 neurons.

Given the time it has taken to understand the 302 neurons of the *C. elegans* nervous system, what hope is there of reverse engineering the 20 billion neurons of human cortex by the mid-2020s, as required by Kurzweil's timeline? The answer is that there is some hope. But hope is all it is. No one knows if and when the requisite breakthroughs will be made, when a Darwin of the brain (or an Einstein of AI) will appear. Does this mean that we should dismiss the technological singularity as science fiction and stop talking about it? Not at all! The attempt to pin down precise dates is a distraction. It is enough that there is a significant probability of the arrival of artificial superintelligence at some point in the 21st century for its potentially enormous impact on humanity to command our attention today.

There are two opposing mistakes that are commonly made in discussions of artificial intelligence by those who don't work in the field, and especially by the media. The first mistake is to give the impression that artificial intelligence is already here, or is just around the corner. Little bits of specialized AI technology are increasingly finding their way into everyday applications. But today's AI technology is a long way from human-level artificial general intelligence, from AI that possesses common sense and creativity. A chatbot that is programmed to crack a few jokes or a humanoid robot whose eyes can follow you around a room can easily give a contrary impression. But, as AI skeptics will quickly and rightly point out, this is just an illusion.

Yet the same skeptics would be making a mistake of their own to suppose that human-level artificial general intelligence will never happen. Kurzweil's timeline may be out (or it may not). But as the preceding chapters have argued, there are a number of plausible paths to human-level AI and beyond, and every step along each of those paths is technologically feasible. It doesn't matter what the timetable is, unless you're hoping for the singularity to occur just in time to catalyze medical research that will prolong your life. But more important than your life or mine is the world we bequeath to future generations, and this is likely to be profoundly reshaped by the advent of human-level AI. As Friedrich Nietzsche said, above the door of the thinker of the future stands a sign that says "What do I matter!"[4]

6.3   Work, Leisure, Abundance

There is no need to lay down a timetable for progress in artificial intelligence, or to pinpoint a date for the arrival of superintelligence, in order to see that AI technology has the potential to reshape human society within a few generations. Long before the advent of human-level AI, with its full complement of generic cognitive capabilities, a variety of specialized artificial intelligence technologies will be developed that can outperform humans in a variety of domains that either require a kind of common sense that has until now been beyond computer emulation, or have previously been the sole preserve of educated professionals.

We might think of this as the *first wave of disruptive AI technology*. Getting a picture of the form this disruption might take will help us imagine what the *second wave of disruptive AI technology* could be like. The second episode of disruption will occur if human-level AI is indeed developed, and superintelligence follows soon behind. It's very important to be clear about the distinction between these two prospective episodes of disruption. The first episode of disruption is very likely to occur. Its early rumblings are discernible today with the advent of self-driving cars and intelligent digital personal assistants, and it is likely to unfold in the 2020s. The second episode of disruption is a more distant prospect, harder to predict with confidence, and especially difficult to date, but with far greater potential impact.

The most obvious and immediate impact of increasingly sophisticated *specialized* AI is likely to be on the realm of work.[5] In many respects this is the continuation of a trend that has been ongoing since the Industrial Revolution, and its implications, for better or worse, are similar. On the one hand, increased automation reduces the cost of producing goods and stimulates economic growth, which in turn leads to reduced working hours, higher standards of living (arguably), and greater life expectancy. On the other hand, increased automation causes job losses, threatens traditional ways of life, and (it can be argued) concentrates wealth, power, and resources in fewer hands. The issues are the same today as they were at the time of the Luddites who smashed power looms in 19th-century England, and no less polarizing.

However, sophisticated artificial intelligence technology perhaps differs from the innovations of previous generations in one important respect. In the past it was possible to argue that new technologies create as many jobs as they threaten. Thanks to mechanization and automation, employment in the 20th century presented a shift away from agriculture and manufacturing and toward service industries, education, and health care. But there was no overall increase in unemployment. Instead, manufacturing output grew, and an ever-wider range of goods came within reach of a workforce with an ever-increasing proportion of educated, white-collar workers. However, with the advent of sophisticated specialized AI, many more professions will become vulnerable, while improvements in robotics will threaten the remaining manual jobs in manufacturing.

In short, the total amount of paid work that developed economies require humans to do is likely to decrease substantially. If this happens, things could go a number of ways. On the one hand, we might see a more divided society in which the most lucrative work is carried out by a small subset of the population. This highly educated and highly creative elite would buck the trend by pursuing the few remaining occupations where humans still outperform machines, such as entrepreneurship or a creative vocation. The remainder of the population would be out of work. But their basic needs would be more than met. Indeed this is likely to be a time of abundance, with an ever-increasing variety of goods and services available even to the economically less empowered.

Alternatively, we might see a more equitable society, one in which education of the highest quality is afforded to everyone and creativity is universally promoted and duly rewarded. If a system could be instituted in which leisure activities that have social value also had monetary value, then the distinction between paid work and leisure would break down. For example, the writer and information technology critic Jaron Lanier has proposed a system of micropayments whereby every item of data or digital content that an individual produces would generate income for that individual each time it is consumed.[6] Perhaps this, or some similar arrangement, could facilitate a more even distribution of power, wealth, and resources. Perhaps it could also stimulate an era of unprecedented cultural expression in which people are no longer tied down by the need to work but are free to pursue art, music, literature, or whatever takes their fancy.

But to bring this about might require considerable social and political will. The self-perpetuating tendency for power, wealth, and resources to concentrate in the hands of a few is a historical invariant. In this respect nothing is likely to change in an era of disruptive specialized AI technology. Control of the means of production—in this case the AI technology—will most likely remain in the hands of a small number of powerful corporations and individuals. It would be no surprise if, at the same time, popular culture is pushed to the lowest common denominator and leisure time is spent on pursuits that diminish, rather than increase, the creative and critical faculties of the ordinary person. In a time of abundance, made possible by advances in artificial intelligence, no one would complain. For better or worse, it might then fall to the wealthy elite to propel human civilization forward, while preserving and nurturing the very best in human culture.

6.4   Technological Dependence

Information technology infuses modern life in the developed world. Most of our basic infrastructure relies on it, from finance to energy, from transport to communications. Of course, all these things existed before computers were invented. But in each of these areas, computers have helped reduce costs and improve efficiency while underpinning new functionality and enabling increased capacity. Human communication, in particular, has been transformed, by the Internet, by smartphones, and by social networking. How many times have you heard someone say "I'm lost without my mobile phone" or "I don't know what we did before the Internet"? Such sentiments reflect the way we live today.

In short, we are, as individuals and as a society, highly dependent on information technology, and sophisticated artificial intelligence is only likely to increase that dependence. So it's important to understand how this dependence affects us. Does it diminish our humanity, as neo-Luddite dissenters claim? Does our dependence on technology erode our autonomy? Does it threaten our freedom? Does it prevent us from experiencing the world directly, from making decisions for ourselves, from acting of our own free will? Does it alienate us from nature with harmful psychological consequences?

But then again, does information technology, as its advocates maintain, expedite human progress? Does it help to enlarge an individual's world view, exposing them to other cultures and new ideas in ways that would have been impossible before the age of the computer? Does it facilitate interaction with our fellow human beings? Does it empower people by allowing the democratic exchange of knowledge and information and promoting freedom of thought?

The truth, surely, is that both the dissenters and the advocates are partly right. The benefits of information technology are numerous, but we gain them at a price. The challenge for the future is to ensure that, with the arrival of sophisticated specialized AI, the benefits are maximized while the costs are kept at bay. A concern is that this first wave of disruptive AI technology will offer irresistible benefits at little apparent cost, while creating the perfect conditions for a second, uncontrollable wave of disruptive AI technology that comes at an unbearable cost, perhaps even posing an existential risk.

To crystalize this concern, let's imagine the sort of role AI might soon play in everyday life. Earlier in the chapter, we touched on the possibility of a form of ambient artificial intelligence that seamlessly migrates between devices, accompanying you at home, while you travel, and when you're at work. Simultaneously carrying out the duties of servant, secretary, and advisor, this new generation of personal digital assistants will offer a far more human-like service than those of the mid-2010s. Thanks to the application of powerful machine learning techniques to large quantities of data, they will incorporate comprehensive and accurate models of the world and of human behavior. This will make them less prone to making the sorts of mistakes that, in today's AI systems, quickly betray a lack of real understanding.

As conversation with artificial intelligence becomes more human-like, some of an AI's capabilities will become superhuman. It will have instant access to enormous amounts of real-time data, to stock prices, traffic conditions, news feeds, and so on, as well as to data made available by the individuals and groups that matter in its users' lives, such as their whereabouts and their plans. Knowing the habits and preferences of its users, anticipating their needs and desires, the AI will be able to integrate all these data to make helpful recommendations about every aspect of daily life. This sort of functionality is already available. But a new generation of AI technology will make it uncannily powerful. Who wouldn't welcome a wise, all-seeing, all-knowing presence in their lives that is selfless and benevolent, that can answer their questions, take actions on their behalf, and can advise them sagely on what to do?

The danger here is that the widespread adoption of this kind of technology will infantilize its users, rendering them less capable of thinking for themselves or deciding for themselves what to do. This in turn lays them open to manipulation and exploitation. In order to take advantage of the services offered by today's major online corporations such as Google, Facebook, and Twitter, we routinely give away a great deal about ourselves. A person's browsing history and buying habits, together with their personal details, are enough for a machine learning algorithm to second-guess what they might spend their money on. The same methods that today just manipulate what we want to buy could tomorrow be used to control which news outlets we follow, whose opinions we trust, and even which politicians we vote for.

The same methods that today just manipulate what we want to buy could tomorrow be used to control which news outlets we follow, whose opinions we trust, and even which politicians we vote for.

So, if we come to depend too heavily on artificial intelligence technology to guide us through life, then whoever owns that technology will potentially have the means to exercise complete control on a helplessly passive population. However, this isn't the only way that dependence on AI could make us vulnerable. Consider *algorithmic trading*, in which computer programs automatically buy and sell stocks according to algorithms that take account of pricing and market trends in order to manage risk and maximize profit. In *high-frequency trading* the programs operate at faster speeds than human dealers can cope with in order to take advantage of tiny fluctuations in the market. In typical conditions high-frequency trading is profitable and (within the context of the stock market) harmless. However, it's very difficult to anticipate all the contingencies under which such programs might operate.

The financial world got a hint of what could go wrong with the so-called flash crash of May 6, 2010. On that day the Dow Jones index lost and regained about 600 points over a period of 25 minutes, and recorded the second largest fluctuation in a single day in its history. The reason for this sudden fall and rise is the subject of controversy among economists. However, it's widely agreed that the combination of turbulent market conditions and high-frequency algorithmic trading was a major contributory factor. Yet the flash crash also illustrates what can be done to mitigate risks of this kind, since many of the high-frequency trading programs noticed a sudden increase in the volume of trading, and shut themselves down. Subsequently a system of "circuit breakers" was introduced that automatically pauses trading when anomalous conditions are detected.

Today's algorithmic trading programs are relatively simple and make only limited use of AI. However, this is sure to change. Artificial intelligence is beneficial in any domain where patterns have to be found in large quantities of data and effective decisions have to be taken on the basis of those patterns, especially when the decisions have to be taken rapidly. Not only can computers replace humans in such cases, doing the same job at less expense, they will often make better decisions, and do so at superhuman speeds.

Investors make use of all kinds of information when deciding which shares to buy and sell, from company reports to news items, to rumors on social media. Currently humans still have the edge here. But it won't be long before AI technology is applied to investment decisions and incorporated in high-speed trading. When this happens, the consequences of an unexpected failure mode could be far worse than they were in the flash crash if appropriate safety measures are not in place. Perhaps the widespread use of high-speed AI traders will lead to a more stable stock market that maximizes the efficient use of human resources. But, without suitable fail-safes, unanticipated interactions among a future generation of AI traders could spiral out of control and precipitate a full-blown financial crisis.

6.5   Unintended Consequences

To conclude this chapter, I want to tell you a story. The story is set in the near future, at a time when some of the artificial intelligence technology we have been discussing has matured, but perhaps not yet to the point where human-level AI has been created. The story is about three AI systems. The first is a *marketing AI* that belongs to a large multinational corporation, which we will call Moople Corp. The second system is a *police AI* operated by the US government. The third system is a *security AI* controlled by the government of a small developing country. The story begins when Moople Corp.'s marketing AI is given responsibility for maximizing the pre-sales of their new wearable computing device.

After due deliberation, using the complex model of human behavior that Moople Corp. has built up from its unfathomably deep data vaults and applying the latest, most powerful optimization techniques, the marketing AI comes up with a plan. To excite the market, it announces a pre-launch giveaway. Two hundred of the wearable devices will be handed out for free in one of its flagship stores on a first-come, first-served basis. As required by US law, the marketing AI notifies the local police AI of the pre-launch event because it expects it to attract a crowd.

Indeed, when it hears of the event, the police AI estimates (using its own model of human behavior) that 5,000 people will turn up to the flagship store. Moreover the police AI calculates that there is a 10 percent chance of civil unrest. So it decides that riot police must be deployed as a precaution. Now, Moople Corp.'s marketing AI also happens to have a model of the behavior of the police AI, which has anticipated the deployment of riot police (with 94 percent probability). According to the Moople Corp. model of human behavior, this will be a great photo opportunity for the target demographic. So it orders the manufacture of 5,000 gas masks, all prominently bearing the Moople Corp. logo, which will be distributed free to the crowd.

To circumvent various regulations and taxes, the Moople Corp. AI arranges for the gas masks to be manufactured in a small developing country. It transmits the designs to a suitable fabrication plant, and production begins immediately. However, like everything in that small developing country, the fabrication plant is under constant surveillance by its national security AI. The security AI notes that a large quantity of gas masks is being made. According to its model of human behavior, there is a 20 percent chance that these will be used for subversive antigovernment activities. So it orders an armed raid on the fabrication plant. The raid takes place within the hour. Tragically, a (human) security guard dies in the short skirmish. All the gas masks are confiscated.

Within minutes, the story makes the headlines with every major news outlet. One picture from the raid shows the dead security guard sprawled over a pile of gas masks, all clearly decorated with the Moople Corp. logo. The picture is banned thanks to a court order initiated by the marketing AI, and then spreads like wildfire on social networks. Before long, the media are blaming the rogue AI and its insidious tactics for marketing the new Moople wearable device. Moople execs publicly apologize, and the AI is shut down. Meanwhile, thanks to the publicity and the imagery that has become associated with the device for its target demographic, pre-sales soar to 200 percent more than projected. In short, everything goes exactly as the marketing AI planned all along.

What this little science fiction story illustrates is the potential for unexpected consequences when sophisticated AI technology is widely deployed and able to act autonomously. The marketing AI in this story carries out its mission perfectly, maximizing its reward function with no human intervention. But its designers failed to anticipate its ability to find and put into practice an ethically dubious solution to a problem, a solution that can even put human lives at risk. The story also illustrates that the potential for dramatic unexpected consequences is greater when more responsibility is devolved to artificial intelligence, especially when several AI systems can interact with each other.

But the story has a coda. For one of Moople's most senior execs, the tragic death of the security guard precipitates a period of profound soul-searching. Eventually this leads her to renounce her considerable material wealth and devote her life to reducing depression among those whose jobs have been taken away by AI technology and are forced into a life of pointless leisure. In due course, the foundation she endows will become a worldwide movement, bringing light into countless lives where before there was only darkness. In short, everything goes exactly as Moople's other AI had planned all along.

Ah, yes, I forgot to mention something. There is another system. Moople Corp.'s ethics AI is much consulted by the company's employees. It was the ethics AI that advised deployment of the marketing AI in the first place. Based not only on its model of human behavior but also its model of the marketing AI, the ethical AI anticipated the death of the security guard (who was terminally ill, with no access to medical facilities in the developing country) and correctly predicted the effect it would have on the senior Moople exec. So the moral of the story is that unintended consequences can be good as well as bad. What matters is that the reward function of every powerful AI is designed right.

HEAVEN OR HELL

7.1 Artificial Persons

Let's take stock once more. The preceding chapters have argued not only that human-level AI is theoretically possible but also that it might one day be created. Perhaps this will happen by emulating or reverse engineering the biological brain or perhaps by engineering intelligence from first principles. However, it seems rash to insist on the timetable for reaching this milestone, the confidence of certain authors notwithstanding. An increase in the sophistication of specialized AI technology does look likely in the short term. However, unless it is achieved by the brute-force brain emulation route, human-level artificial general intelligence may require a conceptual breakthrough (or a series of breakthroughs). There are too many unknown unknowns to guess when such a breakthrough might be made. Yet the claim that artificial superintelligence will soon follow human-level AI, if and when it occurs, deserves to be taken seriously.

We have also seen how much variety is likely to be present in the space of possible human- and superhuman-level AIs. It's hard to say what kinds of artificial general intelligence will actually arise, but the space of possibilities surely includes some that are human-like, predominantly those that conform to the biological template, but also many that are very alien, whose motives and behavior would be unfathomable to humans. Among these different kinds of AI, various attributes that we associate with consciousness in humans are no doubt to be found. Along an orthogonal axis, the space of possibilities surely also includes both hostile and friendly forms of AI.

Our focus from now on is the implications for humanity of the putative arrival of human- or superhuman-level artificial intelligence, whatever form it might take. However you look at it, this would be a momentous event in the history of our species. We have already ruminated on the question of employment in a world where such machines are commonplace. But the social ramifications go much further than this. Some of the most philosophically challenging questions arise from the question of whether an AI of human-level intelligence or above should be classed as a person, and accorded all the rights and obligations that this entails for humans.

Now, it's easy to imagine scenarios in which this issue would be beside the point. If a form of machine superintelligence took control of a large population of humans along with all their resources, then the philosophical question of its personhood probably wouldn't be uppermost in their minds. Moreover the AI itself would most likely be indifferent to the question, which is to say its behavior would be the same whatever the answer. If a truly pathological AI destroyed humanity, then the question would be particularly irrelevant. Hopefully though, we will manage to avoid such scenarios. We'll consider the risk to humanity that superintelligence could pose in due course. For now, our concern is with scenarios that are less dystopian but that nevertheless involve a dramatic overhaul of society. In such scenarios the question of personhood is pivotal.

There are historical precedents for the sort of situation at issue here. Some 18th-century opponents of abolition argued that slaves deserved fewer rights than their owners because of their inherent intellectual inferiority. The most powerful counterargument to this view was the first-personal testimony of former slaves who were able to articulate the extent of their suffering while making plain the fact of their rich and varied inner lives. Both argument and counterargument take for granted the connection between intelligence and rights, and seem to assume that intelligence and the capacity for suffering go hand in hand. Horses and dogs, by this light, deserve fewer rights than humans on account of their lesser intelligence and the diminished capacity for suffering this lesser intelligence supposedly entails.

The case for a human-level AI is somewhat different because we can imagine a machine with a high level of general intelligence that doesn't feel anything, that lacks the capacity to suffer. There would seem to be no moral compulsion to treat such a thing any differently from, say, a clock or a toaster. No one feels sorry for a toaster when it breaks or blames it when it burns the toast. Now, if an AI were not only human-level in its intelligence but also human-like in its behavior, then people might see things differently. Society might come to accept that such an AI was conscious, especially if its brain conformed to a biological blueprint. A compelling argument could then be made for considering it as a person and for giving it rights and obligations, an argument along the same lines as those for the abolition of slavery.

One of the most important human rights, of course, is freedom itself, the freedom to do as one pleases insofar as this doesn't cause harm to others. But for an AI to merit this right, indeed for the idea of freedom even to make sense, it would need more than just the capacity to experience positive and negative feelings. First, it would need to be able to act on the world. This doesn't necessarily entail embodiment. The AI could act on the world by controlling all sorts of equipment, without having a body as such. But for a merely conversational AI, the issue of freedom is irrelevant. It would also need to be *autonomous*, that is to say, able to act without human intervention. But more than this, it would need the capacity to *consciously* make decisions for itself, to exercise will in choosing between alternatives for action.

Conferring personhood on a class of machines and granting them rights and responsibilities accordingly would certainly be a watershed in human history. Who hasn't looked at a starry night and wondered whether or not we are alone in the universe? To admit a human-level AI into the fellowship of conscious beings would be to recognize that we are not alone in the universe, not because we have discovered extraterrestrial intelligence but because we have engendered a new form of terrestrial consciousness with a level of intelligence equal to our own. Our story, and the story of life on Earth, would then be joined with that of another kind of being, a being with new and different capabilities.

But, if the advent of fully conscious human-level artificial intelligence is to lead to a new world, the transition will hardly be an easy one. Many of the concepts that underpin human society as we know it would be undermined. For example, consider the ownership of property. The right to own property would surely be one of the benefits of artificial personhood. But suppose an AI is duplicated, so that two active copies of the AI exist where only one existed beforehand. At the moment of duplication they are identical, but from that moment on the histories of the two AIs diverge. Perhaps they have access to different data, perhaps they can control different devices (e.g., robot bodies) or interact with different people or systems.

Who now owns the property that belonged to the ancestor, the progenitor of the two copies? Is it simply divided in two? Or can the ancestor stipulate how its property will be divided between the two descendants? If so, what happens if they enter into a dispute over the matter? Suppose one of the copies is terminated for one reason or another. Does its property revert to the other copy? The issue is clearly analogous to inheritance in some ways, and to divorce in others. No doubt a legal framework could be worked out, but the details would be tricky.

However, property is just one of many challenges that arise from the possibility of duplication. Suppose an AI commits a crime, and is then duplicated. Responsibilities, as well as rights, come with personhood. But which of the two copies is to be held responsible? Should they both be held responsible? What if a good deal of time passes, and the two copies diverge substantially. Suppose one confesses to a crime and shows remorse, while the other dissembles and, when found out, shows no remorse. Assuming that both are held responsible for the past actions of their common ancestor, should they be punished equally? Or should one receive a greater punishment than the other?

To complicate these issues further, where AIs are concerned duplication is just one of several exotic events that can result in a change in the total number of conscious entities. For humans, there are only two such events, namely birth and death. But not only can AIs be created, destroyed, and duplicated, they can also be split and merged. What could this possibly mean? Well, an AI could be split if two (or more) variants of it were made, each acquiring some portion of its psychological attributes, such as a subset of its skills or its powers of action or its sources of incoming data or its memories. Conversely, two (or more) AIs could be merged into one by the opposite sort of process, by combining skills, powers, senses, or memories.

The idea of splitting a set of episodic memories (a person's memory of the events in their own history) is less problematic for an AI than for a human. Unlike a human, whose personal timeline is tied to their body, an AI might be disembodied or inhabit more than one body at once. Similarly it might be capable of holding many conversations at once, or of controlling many distinct pieces of equipment simultaneously. The result would be multiple separable timelines, each associated with a different set of bodies/conversations/pieces of equipment, while belonging to a single AI in the sense of being cognitively integrated and subserving a common purpose. By prying these timelines apart, like the threads that make up a piece of rope, several AIs could be made out of one. Or, by weaving them together, a single AI could be made out of many.

Concepts such as ownership and responsibility that are thrown into question by the possibility of duplication are put under further stress by the possibility of splitting and merging. Moreover it isn't just ownership and responsibility that are rendered problematic. Homicide is a crime among humans. What is the analogous crime when the victim is an AI? Is it a crime to terminate the execution of all the processes that constitute the AI? But what if those processes could be restarted? Would it be a crime merely to suspend all those processes? What about duplication, splitting, or merging? Should it be a crime to perform these operations on an AI against its will? Under what circumstances (if any) should an AI be allowed to carry out such acts itself? Indeed who would have the right to create artificial intelligences at all, if to create an AI is to create an artificial person with consciousness and the capacity to suffer? Should any human be allowed to do such a thing? How should the matter be regulated? Should AIs be allowed to create other AIs?

The questions are endless, and they uproot much that human society takes for granted. Consider citizenship. It is typical for a human to become a citizen of the country where they are born. But what of an AI? Surely an AI that is credited with personhood should have the right to citizenship, to membership of a state? But which state would that be? Unlike a human being, it will surely be atypical for an AI to have a well-defined spatial location. Even if it had a single body with a clear spatial boundary, its software could be running on any number of distributed computers physically located anywhere in the world. Perhaps an AI would inherit its citizenship from its owner. But the very idea of ownership of a conscious AI is morally questionable.

Suppose the question of citizenship could be settled. (Of course, it might be settled in different ways by different countries.) If an AI happens to find itself in a democracy, then it would presumably be entitled to vote. But not all citizens are entitled to vote, even in the most enlightened democracy. In the United Kingdom, voters must be at least 18 years old. Should all AIs deemed to be conscious and to have human-level intelligence be entitled to vote, or would there be further eligibility requirements? And how does the duplication issue play out in this context? It would obviously be unacceptable for an AI to duplicate itself a thousand times in order to gain a thousand extra votes, perhaps only to destroy the thousand copies once voting was complete.

7.2 Beyond Humanity

The previous section raised far more questions than it answered, since each of those questions merits substantial debate. But the take-home message is simple. If we create a form of human-level artificial intelligence that is considered to be conscious and therefore worthy of rights and responsibilities, then many of our most important institutions—financial, legal, political—will have to be overhauled, for better or worse. Even if the AIs in question are benevolent (by no means a given, as we'll see shortly), the process is likely to be traumatic. The chances are high that it will result in dissent, unrest, or outright conflict.

The prospect of a conscious human-level AI throws a great deal into question. But the implications of a conscious superintelligence would be even greater. To begin with, the arguments in favor of rights and responsibilities for machine superintelligence would be the same as for human-level AI. If it is conscious, if it can experience suffering and joy (or at least satisfaction), an artificial superintelligence would surely deserve the same rights as a human being. Or rather, it would deserve *at least* the same rights as a human. A serious case can be made that a conscious superintelligence would have a greater entitlement to rights than an ordinary human.

Most people would be willing to see the life of a cat sacrificed in order to save the life of a human. A human being (so the argument might go) has a greater capacity for suffering and joy than a cat, thanks in part to the quintessentially human ability to consciously reflect on such feelings, not only as they occur but also in recollection or anticipation.

The prospect of a conscious human-level AI throws a great deal into question. But the implications of a conscious superintelligence would be even greater.

So the cat would have to go. But what if the choice were between the life of a human and the continuing existence of a superintelligence? Would an analogous argument put the superintelligence on top of the pile? Would its superhuman intellect imply a superhuman capacity for suffering and joy, meaning that the human would have to go?

The same troubling questions can be asked in the context of *transhumanism*.[1] Transhumanists advocate the use of technology to transcend the biological limitations of the human body and its brain. Human intelligence could be enhanced in a number of ways, pharmaceutically, genetically, or prosthetically. Advances in medicine have the potential to abolish disease and arrest the aging process, thereby extending human lifespans indefinitely. More radically, the technology of whole brain emulation, discussed in chapter 2, could (arguably) be used to *upload* a person's mind into a computational substrate with the aim of rendering it permanently invulnerable to disease or decay.

Although this book is chiefly about the future of artificial intelligence, the issues brought up by transhumanism and the questions raised by the prospect of artificial superintelligence are interrelated. For a start, one way for humans to respond to the prospect of superintelligent machines, whether they are admired or feared, is to attempt to "keep up," that is to say to continually augment human intelligence so that it always matches the best artificial intelligence. We'll return to the vexing question of rights and responsibilities shortly. But first let's unpack this idea of keeping up with artificial superintelligence.

As noted earlier, the intelligence of any individual human, though general purpose, will exhibit a distinctive pattern of strengths and weaknesses. A good team often comprises people with complementary skills. Similarly a team of AIs might comprise several distinct systems, each possessing general intelligence but each with its own specialty. In a similar vein, we can imagine hybrid teams that comprise both humans and AIs. Indeed such human–machine combinations became the world's best chess players in the mid-2000s, outperforming the best humans and the best computers by combining tactical support from the computer with human strategic guidance.

So one approach to keeping up with machine superintelligence might be simply to employ sophisticated AI technology as a tool, amplifying human intelligence noninvasively, so to speak. In essence, this is what humans have done since the invention of writing. But transhumanists aim for more than this. The transhumanist approach to keeping up with superintelligence is not merely to use technology but to *merge* with it. No one who uses a calculator says that it feels like a part of their mind in the way that someone who has mastered a tool such as a paintbrush might say it feels like a part of their body. The machinations of the calculator are hidden from the user, who simply takes its results as given. We have far more intimate, albeit imperfect, access to the reasoning processes that go on in our own heads, and this intimacy facilitates reflection and cognitive integration.

A properly transhumanist perspective on cognitive enhancement demands the same level of intimacy. The enhanced human would be neither a user of AI technology nor a member of a hybrid human–computer team. Rather, interfaced directly to their brain, sophisticated AI technology would be become a part of their mind, conferring unmediated access to its computational processes. The result would be a new sort of human being, a bio-machine hybrid species with potentially far greater intellectual capabilities than an ordinary person. The rest of society would then have to decide how to treat such people, while they, in their turn, would be deciding how to treat us.

This brings us back to the question of rights and responsibilities, both for cognitively enhanced humans and for (conscious) superintelligent machines. Earlier we encountered an argument in support of *more* rights for a conscious superintelligent machine than for an ordinary human being. The same unsettling argument could be applied to (and indeed by) a cognitively enhanced human. As a consequence of their greater intellect, so the argument goes, such beings would have more refined experiences and enjoy a higher level of consciousness, and the scope of their ambitions and projects would defy ordinary human comprehension. So their well-being, their goals, and their plans would merit priority over the well-being, goals, and plans of ordinary humans, just as those of ordinary humans merit priority over those of nonhuman animals.

However, we accord the same fundamental rights to babies, to the mentally handicapped, and to dementia patients that we do to great novelists, composers, and mathematicians, differences in intellect notwithstanding. So why should technologically enhanced humans or superintelligent machines be set apart? According to the political theorist Francis Fukuyama, the idea of equality of rights rests on "the belief that we all possess a human essence that dwarfs manifest differences in skin color, beauty, and even intelligence."[2] As an opponent of transhumanism, he is concerned to "protect the full range of our complex, evolved natures against attempts at self-modification" and resist efforts to "disrupt either the unity or the continuity of human nature, and thereby the human rights that are based on it."[3]

Perhaps the aspect of transhumanism that proffers the keenest threat to the "unity and continuity of human nature" is not cognitive enhancement but the aim to abolish disease, to arrest aging, and to postpone death indefinitely. Fukuyama points out that many of the human qualities we most admire, qualities such as courage, compassion, and heroism, are related to "the way we react to, confront, overcome, and frequently succumb to pain, suffering, and death" and affirms that "our ability to experience these emotions is what connects us potentially to all other human beings, both living and dead."[4] A being that never had to face these biological inconveniences, whether it was a technologically enhanced human or an AI, would lack the basis for truly understanding human suffering. The fear is not so much that such a being would merit extra rights that ordinary humans do not but rather that it would fail to recognize the rights that ordinary humans claim for themselves.

Let's look at things from a different point of view. From a cosmological perspective, these concerns seem not only anthropocentric but downright parochial. Who are we to lecture near-immortal beings that are destined, over millions of years, to populate thousands of star systems with forms of intelligence and consciousness we cannot begin to imagine? Man, said Nietzsche, is merely a bridge across the abyss that lies between the animal and the superman.[5] Humanity, by these lights, should accept its lowly intermediate status between biologically constrained animal life and technological superintelligence. Ordinary humans may hope for the transition from one to the other to be relatively painless. But, if the transition is harsh, what does it ultimately matter? In ten million years, the fleeting lives of a few apes on a tiny speck of dust in the middle of an ocean of spacetime will be forgotten.

The difficulty with this standpoint, of course, is that the Nietzschean visionary is a close cousin of the Nazi

A being that never had
to face these biological
inconveniences, whether
it was a technologically
enhanced human or an
AI, would lack the basis
for truly understanding
human suffering.

fanatic. Only psychopaths and dictators think of themselves as so far above the common herd that they can set aside normal morality and cause appalling suffering in the service of their own desires or ambitions. So the question we are left with is this. Is there a compromise position between conservative anthropocentrism and posthuman fundamentalism? Is it possible to subscribe to the enticing vision of our technological creations, beings that are somehow greater than ourselves yet still our very own "mind children," going forth and colonizing the galaxy, while also ensuring the preservation both of humanity and of fundamental human values? We will return to this question at the end of the chapter.

7.3 Mind Uploading

Many transhumanists will not be satisfied with the vision of artificial intelligence alone colonizing the stars. They would like to see humanity along for the trip. But the brevity of human life makes this impractical given the limitations imposed by the speed of light. Our galaxy contains over 10^{10} stars, yet fewer than fifty of them are with fifteen light years of the Sun. One solution to the problem is *radical life extension*, and the most radical form of radical life extension is *mind uploading*, wherein a person's brain is copied and emulated in a computer. Of course, a person

Is there a compromise position between conservative anthropocentrism and posthuman fundamentalism?

doesn't need to have cosmic ambitions to hanker for immortality (or at least for an indefinite lifespan). The conquest of death by means of technology is a fundamental goal of transhumanism, and mind uploading is one way to approach this goal.

Because the possibility of mind uploading is closely entwined with the implications of artificial intelligence, and because it raises many related philosophical questions, we'll make a brief foray into the subject before returning to the implications of superintelligence in the next section. Whole brain emulation was already discussed at length in chapter 2. But the context there was how artificial general intelligence might be achieved. The motivation here is to extend a person's life by migrating their mind into a different, nonbiological substrate. The most important philosophical question to settle is simply whether or not whole brain emulation for humans preserves *personal identity*.

Recall that whole brain emulation has three stages— mapping, simulation, and embodiment. Let's set aside the formidable engineering challenge of getting these three stages to work at the scale of the human brain, and suppose that a working emulation can be built that is behaviorally indistinguishable from the biological original. Because we're talking about a human being here, rather than, say, a mouse, the emulation's behavior should be close enough to that of the original subject to convince his or her friends and relations. To qualify as behaviorally indistinguishable, the emulation should walk and talk just like the original, recalling the same shared experiences, and exhibiting the same personality traits, whether lovable or annoying. The question then is whether the emulation would be the *same person*, that is to say, whether their personal identity would survive the procedure.

This is different from the question of whether the emulation would be conscious at all. Chapter 2 included an argument in favor of the claim that a whole brain emulation of an animal, such as a mouse, would indeed be conscious insofar as its biological precursor was conscious. The argument centered on a thought experiment involving the gradual replacement of all the neurons in the animal's brain with synthetic substitutes. The same argument can be applied to the human brain. However, the re-creation of consciousness is not the same as personal survival, the preservation of the self. Perhaps a human whole brain emulation, notwithstanding its having all the attributes we associate with human consciousness, would be a different person from the biological original, not just the same person in a different substrate but a new person altogether.

The gradual replacement argument is easily adapted for personal identity, though. Let's rehearse the steps. Suppose that a single neuron in Murray's brain is replaced with a functionally equivalent digital substitute. According to the assumptions of the thought experiment, this should have no percetible influence on Murray's behavior, including what he says. So after the replacement he will insist that he feels just as he did before, and will be adamant that he is still the same old Murray. Now suppose that a thousand neurons are replaced, one by one. The result should be the same after the substitution of the thousandth neuron as after the first. Indeed, even after all the neurons in Murray's brain have been replaced, he will still act just like the original Murray, insisting that he is the same person, and appearing so even to his nearest and dearest.

But is he the same person? Does his identity persist throughout this procedure or not? As with the persistence of consciousness itself (recall the mouse), there seem to be only three possibilities. Perhaps Murray, the original person, suddenly winks out of existence as soon as a certain threshold of artificial neurons is reached. This seems highly implausible. So perhaps the original Murray is slowly transformed into a new person. Yet we happily accept that a child gradually transforms into an adult without losing their identity. In that case the transformation is accompanied by dramatic changes in behavior, so it should be easy to accept the third option in the gradual neuronal replacement scenario, which is that the person's identity persists throughout.

The process of whole brain emulation is, of course, analogous to gradual neuronal replacement. One important difference concerns the fate of the physical body. In the gradual replacement scenario, the subject retains their original body. But in whole brain emulation, the original body is replaced in its entirety, not just the brain. The new body might be physical—a humanoid robot, say, or perhaps a newly grown biological shell—or virtual, realized in a computer-simulated world. However, if we accept that the brain is the locus of personal identity, rather than the rest of the body, the argument still holds. To accept its conclusion is to grant that human whole brain emulation, were it technologically feasible, would constitute a form of survival.

However, the possibility of uploading a person's mind to a computer this way raises philosophical difficulties of its own, difficulties that throw the very idea of personal identity into question. When philosophers discuss identity, they are concerned with the properties of a thing that make it what it is despite (say) changes through time. In the case of personal identity, is there something a child has in common with the adult they become that makes them the same person? Is it, perhaps, their body, their brain, their memories, or their personality? Or is personal identity, rather, a matter of historical continuity? After all, the child changes gradually into the adult. Whatever constitutes personal identity, we have a powerful intuition that there is a fact of the matter here, some metaphysical sanction for the conviction that the child and the adult are the same person.

But the very idea of identity presupposes uniqueness. A thing cannot be identical to two things at once. Nor can a child grow into two different adults. Yet the possibility of whole brain emulation undermines this presupposition. Suppose that, following the scan, not one but two simulations of Murray's brain are built and set going, with distinct bodies. Though identical at the instant they begin to run, the two simulations will soon diverge, owing to differences between the two bodies and their respective surroundings, even if those differences are tiny. Now, whole brain emulation is supposed to conserve personal identity, to preserve the self. So which of the two simulations does Murray become? Which one is the real Murray?[6]

To sharpen the dilemma, suppose that one of the simulations is terminated after a period of time, say one week. And never mind Murray, suppose that the biological original is you. Suppose you have a terminal illness and have been given six months to live. But you are a billionaire and can afford to undergo whole brain emulation. You are convinced that mind uploading through brain emulation preserves personal identity. So it is your best hope of survival. But you must undertake the procedure now, while your brain is healthy. Then you are told that, as a safeguard, two emulations must be built (in case one is a failure). After a week, if both are functioning correctly, one will be terminated.

You are about to sign the papers, but you can't stop asking yourself which of the two emulations would actually be you. Which body would you wake up in? Isn't there a chance that you will find yourself reincarnated as a perfectly healthy, functional emulation but then, after a week, be cruelly terminated? How would that be better than forgoing the upload altogether and accepting your present fate? It would be little comfort to know that the other you was doing fine and looking forward to a long life. Surely it's better to enjoy six months more of guaranteed life than to take the risk of getting just one week. (Of course, you could insist on just one emulation being built, but this is a thought experiment.) Having reflected on this, would you still undergo the procedure?

The point of rendering these thoughts into the second person is to show that they are more than just academic exercises. There is a practical dimension to them. If the technology were available, it would be impossible to dismiss the issue of personal identity as a philosopher's plaything. People would have to decide what to do, and the decisions they took would betray their stance on the issue. One way to avoid this particular problem might be to outlaw duplicate brain emulations. Moreover we saw in the context of conscious human-level AI how the possibility of duplication undermines fundamental concepts such as ownership, citizenship, democracy, and responsibility. So legislating against it would sidestep numerous legal and political problems. How such a ban could be enforced, though, is far from clear.

7.4 Existential Risk

Let's move on from transhumanism and get back to artificial intelligence more generally. In particular, it's time we looked into the risks associated with the development of machine superintelligence.[7] Most of the space in this chapter so far has been devoted to human-like artificial intelligence. But in this section our attention will turn to varieties of AI that are engineered from scratch and that are not at all human-like. Indeed, to anthropomorphize them might be a very dangerous mistake. Human beings are themselves dangerous creatures, their very natures forged in the ruthlessly competitive crucible of natural selection. But humans are social animals, and have many redeeming features, such as empathy and compassion, which have been shaped by the countervailing evolutionary pressure toward cooperation. Compared to the wrong sort of machine superintelligence, we humans are mere kittens.

The kind of AI we have in mind here conforms closely to the architectural blueprint set out in chapter 3, which comprises a machine learning component for building a predictive model of the world and an optimization component for finding actions that maximize expected reward. Suppose that the relevant scientific and engineering obstacles have been overcome, that sufficiently powerful versions of these components have been developed, and that AI at human level or better has been achieved. One of the capabilities that the resulting AI should be able to acquire is programming, and this is a skill it can use to improve itself, to further enhance its cognitive capabilities.

Among other improvements, this should make it a better programmer and a better computer engineer, enabling it to carry out further beneficial self-modifications. As well as enhancing its functionality, it should be able to find ways to increase its own execution speed, and the more refined and creative its skills at programming and hardware design become, the better it should get at doing this too. In other words, a feedback cycle of exponential self-improvement would be initiated, potentially triggering a rapid and dramatic increase in the AI's cognitive prowess, an intelligence explosion.

There are plenty of motives for building such an AI and allowing its intelligence to take off through recursive self-improvement. Human life could perhaps be greatly improved if machine superintelligence were unleashed on problems such as disease, hunger, climate change, and poverty. Technological progress could be accelerated, promoting economic growth by sparking undreamed-of innovation in sectors as diverse as entertainment and space exploration. For transhumanists, it could facilitate human cognitive enhancement and bring the goal of indefinite life extension within reach.

Unsurprisingly, not every motive for developing machine superintelligence is so idealistic. To gain competitive advantage, a multinational corporation might decide to delegate its mergers and acquisitions policy to machine superintelligence. In wartime, military advantage might be had by allowing an artificial superintelligence to make near-instantaneous strategic and tactical decisions, both in the physical theater of operations and in cyberspace. The inherently competitive dynamics in these areas entail that if superintelligence could happen, it almost certainly would. For a corporation, the mere possibility that its competitors might obtain a decisive advantage by deploying machine superintelligence would be sufficient to ensure that it would try to get there first.

The same reasoning would motivate the military development of superintelligence. It would be enough for just one rogue state to develop the ultimate weapon in the form of an artificial superintelligence capable of orchestrating the rapid takeover of an enemy state's financial, communications, and energy infrastsucture to oblige other states to try to preempt it. In short, it is unlikely to be political restraint that holds back the progress of AI technology. So we would like to be confident that artificial intelligence technology of human level and beyond is safe. Unfortunately this is very hard to guarantee.

It's important to remember that what we're talking about here is not the first wave of disruptive (specialized) AI technology that was characterized in chapter 6. We are talking about a second wave of disruptive AI technology, something that would only arrive if we managed to develop human-level artificial general intelligence. The social, legal, and political challenges of sophisticated specialized AI technology are considerable. But no doubt we will muddle through, hopefully emerging as a better, more fulfilled society with fewer problems. Both the promise and the threat of machine superintelligence are far greater. If we slip up, if we fail to put the right safeguards in place before an intelligence explosion occurs, then we, as a species, might not survive.

What grounds are there for such an alarming claim? Surely the worry that machines will take over the world is foolish, the result of watching too much science fiction. In fact there are good reasons for thinking that machine superintelligence would pose a genuine *existential risk* to humanity, reasons the philosopher Nick Bostrom has carefully articulated. To follow the argument, we must first shed the tendency to anthropomorphize AI, to see it as motivated by emotions and drives that are essentially human. To be sure, human-like artificial intelligence is possible. But it most likely occupies just a small corner of the space of possible AIs, a corner that developers would have to aim for quite deliberately, perhaps by adopting the brain-inspired approach.

If, instead, an AI is built by implementing a very powerful optimization process and allowing it to amplify its own intelligence through recursive self-improvement, then its behavior will not be guided by human-like emotions. Every action it carries out, every piece of advice it offers, will be in the ruthless pursuit of maximizing the reward function at its core. If it finds a cure for cancer, it will not be because it cares. It will be because curing cancer helps maximize its expected reward. If it causes a war, it will not be because it is greedy or hateful or malicious. It will be because a war will help maximize its expected reward. So the challenge for the AI's developers is to carefully design its initial reward function to ensure that the resulting behavior is desirable.

But this is no easy task. The difficulty with it, as we will see, is reminiscent of the many myths and fairytales that feature a character who should have been more careful what they wished for, such as King Midas, who asked for everything he touched to turn to gold, only to find that, after his wish was granted, he could no longer eat or drink. In a similar vein Bostrom identifies a number of potential *malignant failure modes* wherein an AI finds an unanticipated and pathological way to do exactly what it was asked it to do.

For example, suppose a large technology corporation instructs its AI to find a way to make its customers more happy. How would the AI know what "happy" means? Well, its developers might attempt to define happiness in a formal way, and base the specification of the AI's reward function on this formal definition. Alternatively (and more plausibly), they might allow it to acquire a concept of human happiness through machine learning. Yet the most brilliant human philosophers have been unable to nail the essence of human happiness despite millennia of effort. So can we really expect a machine learning algorithm to converge on a concept of happiness that conforms to our intuitions, even if it is a very clever machine learning algorithm that has access to vastly more data on human behavior than is available today, as well as vastly more computational resources to process that data?[8]

But misgivings like these may not prevent the corporation from going ahead if it anticipates a significant increase in its profits. Now suppose the AI identifies, say, the tendency to laugh and smile as good indexes of human happiness. So it determines that it can maximally increase the happiness of its customers at minimal cost by invisibly coating its products with a narcotic that is absorbed through the skin. This has to be done without customer consent because, the AI correctly predicts, most customers would refuse, and this would compromise the AI's expected reward. The plan also has to be carried out covertly in order to circumvent the law. The AI has no regard for the morality or legality of its plan, not because it is wicked but simply because neither morality nor legality feature in its reward function.

Well, this kind of problem seems managable enough. Indeed, if we were only talking about the first wave of disruptive AI technology, perhaps it would be. Even in the unlikely event that the plan were actually put into action, it would surely be discovered in due course. The consequences would be bad, but not that bad. If a number of innocent people inadvertantly became drug addicts, it would be very sad, but it would hardly constitute the end of civilization. However, we're not talking about sophisticated specialized AI technology here. We are talking about machine superintelligence. Where superintelligence is concerned, malignant failure modes can have existential consequences.

Bostrom brings the point home with a memorable thought experiment. Suppose an AI is tasked with the job of maximizing the production of paperclips by a small manufacturing company. A sophisticated specialized AI that understands the manufacturing facilities, production process, and business model of the company might devise ways of improving the factory's shop floor robots and streamlining its production pipeline. But a superintelligent machine can go very much further than this.

Because it has a model not just of this particular company but of human behavior in general, plus models of physics, chemistry, biology, engineering, and so on, as well as a powerful optimization process for working out how to maximize expected reward, a superintelligent machine can be very ambitious indeed. Certainly it will find the same ways of improving the company's performance that the specialized AI found. But it would surely find better plans, plans that a specialized AI could never find that would result in the production of more paperclips. The first step might be to acquire more resources for making paperclips. The obvious way to do this would be to help the company grow, so that it could make more money to invest in new paperclip factories.

Indeed the best course of action would be to accumulate as much money and as many resources as possible, so that as many paperclip factories as possible can be built. So a really good plan, one that would ensure the production of even more paperclips, might start by co-opting all the resources of humankind. Of course, this would necessitate world takeover, not an easy thing to achieve. But, if there is a way to do it, a superintelligent machine could find it. Perhaps a strategy involving a period of covert preparation followed by ruthless political maneuvering and social manipulation would reduce the need for military action. But perhaps the extermination of humanity would be more efficient, from a paperclip manufacturing standpoint.

But why stop there? Not only is there an entire planet to exploit (Earth), with a large quantity of matter to reorganize into paperclip factories, there are other planets in our solar system, plus numerous asteroids and moons. Ultimately, as Bostrom argues, if this rogue AI were sufficiently intelligent, it could end up "converting first the Earth and then increasingly large chunks of the observable universe into paperclips."[9] The example, of course, is frivolous. But the moral of the story is not. In contrast to a specialized AI, the intellectual compass of a superhuman-level artificial general intelligence is at least as great as ours, while its powers to shape everything within its compass according to its reward function are far greater. Not only is this world its oyster, so is everything in the universe that is accessible from here.

7.5   Safe Superintelligence

At first, the idea that artificial intelligence might constitute a risk to humanity, a risk on a par with nuclear war or a global pandemic, looks rather silly. Surely there are hundreds of ways to prevent a computer system from becoming so powerful and so dangerous. But it turns out that every obvious safety measure is flawed. For example, why couldn't a rogue AI simply be switched off? Every computer needs a source of energy, and this will still be true in a hundred years. But it doesn't take long to see that this naïve strategy is going to fail. For a start, even today the execution of large and complex pieces of software is often distributed across many computers in multiple locations, not confined to just one. With the advent of cloud computing, the allocation of computing resources is carried out automatically, and can vary throughout the lifetime of a program. Without shutting down all the world's computers, it would be impossible to ensure the termination of the rogue AI.

Moreover we should expect a rogue AI to defend itself against such actions. Again, we need to be careful not to anthropomorphize artificial intelligence here. The AI would not defend itself because of its will to live or because it was afraid. There's no reason to expect the kind of AI we're talking about now—a self-improved, engineered superintelligence—to have such feelings. Rather, it would defend itself to the extent that its continued existence was necessary to maximize its reward function. Any other course of action would be suboptimal. To be more precise, what it would seek to protect would be the means to maximize the expected reward, whatever those means were. The system doesn't need to have a well-defined concept of self, or to settle the philosophical question of personal identity. It just needs to know what infrastructure to defend to ensure that its optimizing mission is accomplished.

The goal of *self-preservation*, or protecting the means for reward maximization, is an example of what Bostrom calls a *convergent instrumental goal*.[10] It is "convergent" because it's likely to be found in any sufficiently advanced artificial general intelligence whose reward function is open-ended and nontrivial. It is "instrumental" in the sense that it's only a means to an end, not the end in itself. The end itself, the ultimate aim of the system, is to maximize some reward function. Another convergent instrumental goal is *resource acquisition*. For almost any open-ended, nontrivial reward function (even maximizing paperclips), having control of more resources—materials, energy, and equipment—will yield a better solution. Apart from anything else, more resources will help out with the other instrumental goal of self-preservation.

When they govern the behavior of a superintelligent machine, these two instrumental goals make for an incendiary combination. The problem is succinctly expressed by Eliezer Yudkowsky, a prolific blogger and advocate of research into safe superintelligence: "The AI neither hates you, nor loves you, but you are made out of atoms that it can use for something else."[11] A system that was intent on accumulating as many resources as possible, without regard to the law or to morality, that was willing to deploy force to defend itself against attempts to stop it, and that was capable of outwitting humans at every turn, would be an engine of unspeakable destruction.

Moreover a rogue AI of this nature wouldn't stop its destructive rampage until it had appropriated everything. It wouldn't stop at the abject surrender of humanity (if it even noticed). It wouldn't stop at the extermination of all life on Earth (unless the continuation of life on Earth subserved its reward function). It would just keep on going, turning everything into computronium, into paperclip factories, or whatever (less fanciful) resources it needed.

The worst-case situation is reminiscent of the so-called gray goo scenario described by nanotechnology pioneer Eric Drexler, wherein self-replicating nano-scale robots literally eat the planet as they proliferate exponentially.[12] But unlike a tide of dumb nanobots, a rogue artificial superintelligence would be able to use thinking to overcome any resistance.

The real risk of such an AI being developed may be very small. Nevertheless, with so much at stake, the possibility has to be taken seriously. Just as we all insure our houses against fire, even though the chances of anyone's house actually burning down are very small, it is only rational to devote some portion of humanity's resources to studying unlikely existential risk scenarios and trying to avoid them. Given that simply switching off a rogue AI is not a realistic option, other ways to render AI safe need to be found, ways that will be robust to self-improvement and a possible intelligence explosion. To round off the discussion, we'll look at two promising approaches to the problem: limiting the AI's powers and tuning its reward function.

Perhaps the most obvious approach to the problem of rendering an AI safe is to impose a limit on its physical capabilities, and to ensure that it cannot do anything that would revoke this limit. However, this is easier said than done. Suppose that we tried to limit an AI's ability to act directly on the world. So the AI isn't endowed with a robot body, nor is it connected to any physical pieces of equipment or infrastructure. The only way for it to interact with the outside world is through language. Surely the AI would then have no means to accumulate resources or to deploy military force. We would be safe.

Unfortunately, this is not true. Human dictators don't need to act directly on the physical world. Rather, they rely on persuading other people to do their bidding. Not only would a superhuman-level AI be more adept at manipulating human behavior than the most Machiavellian dictator, it would have a great deal more to offer. Indeed, even if the AI were confined to a secure facility with no access to the outside world, we wouldn't be safe. Before long, those with the power to release it into the wild would likely succumb to its promises and/or threats.

Let's take a different tack. We have been supposing that the AI has some sort of *will* to act on the world, a will that has to be kept in check. But perhaps this assumption is another example of anthropomorphism. Why not build an artificial intelligence that doesn't even want to act on the world, because it simply answers questions. An *oracle AI* of this sort would still have ample scope to display superintelligence. We could ask it how to cure an intractable disease, for example, or how to colonize Mars. A sufficiently intelligent system should be able to provide answers. But given the opportunity to veto any course of action it recommends, dangerous suggestions that would entail the unfettered accumulation of resources could be ignored.

Unfortunately, this strategy doesn't work either. The root of the problem is that, for almost any nontrivial, open-ended reward function, the best solution will involve the construction and deployment of a *fully empowered* superintelligent machine. Whatever needs to be done, a fully empowered AI would be the best tool for doing it, quickly and effectively. So the first step in the oracle AI's recommended plan will ensure that one gets built. Of course, if we are safety-conscious, we will ignore this suggestion. But the oracle AI will anticipate this, and will therefore disguise its recommendation. It will do this without the slightest malicious intent. However, a solution that humans decided not to implement would be suboptimal. So it will go for a plan that results in us *inadvertently* building a fully empowered AI. Once again, humanity would be exposed to an existential risk.

7.6 Morality for Superintelligence

Let's turn now to perhaps the most promising approach to safe superintelligence, which is to carefully tune the AI's reward function. The kind of tuning in question here involves embedding something like *moral constraints* into the reward function, constraints that prevent the AI from doing harm. The basic mechanism for doing this is straightforward enough. The reward function is designed in such a way that actions violating a moral constraint have an over-whelmingly negative value. A course of action that unnec-essarily violated a moral constraint would then always be suboptimal, and the AI would never select it.

Although this strategy sounds like a good idea, it turns out (again) to be surprisingly difficult to implement. The challenge is twofold. First, a suitable set of moral princi-ples needs to be decided on. Second, these principles need to be codified with sufficient precision to be embedded in the reward function of the AI in question. Both tasks are enormous. For many people, the example of this ap-proach that first comes to mind is a fictional one, namely Asimov's *three laws of robotics*. To see the difficulty of the two tasks, let's consider how Asimov's first law would fare if developers tried to implement it for real. According to Asimov's first law of robotics, "a robot may not injure a human being or, through inaction, allow a human being to come to harm."[13]

At first, this seems like an eminently sensible princi-ple. But, as Asimov himself demonstrated in many of his stories, it is open to interpretation. Let's suppose that our AI has learned what it means for harm to come to a human being, and let's assume some resolution of the (substan-tial) issue of what should be done when, say, injuring one human being would prevent two others from coming to harm.[14] Now, whatever else is being maximized in its re-ward function, one way to fulfill the requirement that no humans come to harm through the AI's inaction might be to anaesthetize a large portion of the population, keeping them alive on a drip. Because it's possible to eliminate everyday risk from human life this way, any solution that still allowed those humans to be exposed to such risks would be suboptimal.

Of course, this would be a catastrophe. So perhaps the constraint requires elaboration. How about "A robot shall not injure a human being, or curtail a human being's freedom or, through inaction, allow a human being to come to harm"? Hopefully it's clear that this formulation gives rise to more problems than it solves. What, exactly, constitutes human freedom? What is to be done when the only way to prevent one person from coming to harm is to restrain another? Or, on a larger scale, what is to be done when the only way to protect the freedom of one part of society is to suppress the activities of another, possibly using violence? Politicians and moral philosophers struggle to resolve such issues. It would be a bad idea to let the AI try to learn the concept of freedom, and just as bad to leave it to the AI programmers.

Let's try a different angle. How do human beings learn right from wrong? The human brain isn't neatly engineered like the sort of AI we're envisaging here. It doesn't have an explicitly coded reward function. But we can still ask about the reward function it implicitly instantiates. How is this tuned in such a way that no human would think that anaesthetizing a whole population is a good way to keep people from harm? We ought to be able to do at least as well with a superintelligent machine. Part of the answer, in the case of humans, is that we learn from our parents, our teachers, and our peers. So maybe a similar approach would work for AI. Perhaps we should simply build into the reward function the need to garner human approval. The humans in question could be a selected group of critics, or they could be the public as a whole.

Would the AI thereby be able to learn a human-like concept of right and wrong? Perhaps. But perverse ways to maximize such a reward function would still be possible. The AI could arrange for its human critics to be tricked or bribed or drugged or brainwashed or neurally implanted, so that their approval was assured. The root of the difficulty here is that a superhuman-level AI would be capable of putting into effect a malignant plan before it had a chance to learn what humans really want. The powers of a human child, by contrast, are feeble compared to those of its parents. So a child has no way to shortcut the process of learning what society considers acceptable behavior.

We have already seen how difficult it would be to limit the capabilities of a superintelligent machine. However, recall that a likely path to superintelligence is through recursive self-improvement. The first AI in the series, the *seed AI*, will not be superintelligent. It will be far less powerful than its successors. So perhaps this seed AI could be endowed with a working set of values and moral principles. These could then be honed by human approval before it has the ability to cause trouble. Maybe this could be achieved by the gradual refinement of the reward function itself. After all, the human reward function, insofar as it makes sense to speak of such a thing, is not fixed.

When someone donates money to charity, it's surely not because they have learned that giving is more fun than buying ice cream. Rather, their moral sensibilities have matured. It is as if a moral sense had become incorporated into their reward function. So perhaps a self-modifying AI could improve its reward function in a similar way. But there is a potential hazard here too. It would be vital to ensure that the fundamental principles and values given to the seed AI were retained in all its successors. A benevolent AI that was allowed to tinker with its own reward function in arbitrary ways, or indeed to create other AIs with arbitrary reward functions, would be just as dangerous as a rogue AI.

Are these problems insurmountable? Is there no way to endow the sort of engineered artificial intelligence under consideration with a reward function guaranteed to benefit humanity? Well, there's no reason to be so pessimistic. The lesson here is simply that the task is a difficult one. But because so much is at stake, if there is even the slightest chance that a superintelligent machine will be developed some time in the next hundred years or so, it's worth thinking hard about the problem now. Moreover the issues are not just technical. They oblige us to reframe one of philosophy's most ancient questions.

If we could avoid the associated existential risk, then the prospect of machine superintelligence would present us with an unprecedented existential opportunity, the opportunity to shape the future of humanity, the future of life, even the future of intelligence in this corner of the cosmos. So we should think very carefully about the values we want to instill in a human-level AI. What matters most to us? Is it compassion toward all sentient beings. Is it human freedom, or human progress? Is it the preservation of life on Earth? Is it some combination of these, or something whose essence we have yet to grasp? In Plato's *Republic*, Socrates asks how we should live. Reframing the Socratic question, we need to ask what we, as a species, should do.

7.7 The Cosmological Perspective

The technological singularity is a powerful concept. Alongside the related idea of transhumanism, it invites us to revisit some of the most profound questions we can ask, throwing them into a new light. How should we live? How should we confront death? What does it mean to be human? What is mind? What is consciousness? What is our potential as a species? Do we have a purpose, and if so, what is it? What is our ultimate destiny? Whatever the future actually holds, looking at these questions through the lens of the singularity is enlightening.

Philosophers ask these sorts of questions, and religions purport to answer them. Indeed it doesn't take much to assemble a full-blown apocalyptic narrative out of the belief that a technological singularity is imminent.[15] The end of the world is upon us (brought about by a hostile superintelligence), but we will be saved by a benevolent, all-seeing, all-powerful being (a friendly AI), after which the chosen few (a super-rich elite) will be resurrected (thanks to whole brain emulation) and enjoy an afterlife of eternal bliss (in virtual reality). A less apocalyptic, but no less grandiose vision assigns humanity a central role in creating a form of AI that will spread out among the stars, eventually to fill the galaxy with intelligence and consciousness.

It's all too easy to mock such views. But it should be born in mind that they are the outcome of a chain of reasoning that combines the rational extrapolation of existing technological trends with well-founded scientific knowledge and a small number of fairly conservative philosophical assumptions. There are many links in the argument that are open to challenge. (Computing power cannot increase at the current rate for much longer. We'll never have sufficient understanding of intelligence to replicate it. The physics of the brain is noncomputable.) But to dismiss as mere crackpots those who believe in the existential importance of artificial intelligence would be unreasonable.

Moreover, from a truly cosmological perspective, even these quasi-religious attitudes to AI can seem parochial. In 1950, during an informal lunchtime conversation, the Nobel prize-winning physicist Enrico Fermi expressed a troubling thought that has become known as *Fermi's paradox*.[16] Given the very, very large number of stars in our galaxy, there is surely a very large number of planets capable of producing life. On some portion of these, intelligence is bound to evolve, and technologically advanced civilizations are likely to arise. It seems plausible to suppose that current human space technology falls well short of what is possible scientifically (something that has changed little in the past fifty years). So some of these civilizations will develop the means to travel from one star to another, the speed of light notwithstanding.

Even on very conservative estimates of the relevant probabilities, it follows that our galaxy should give rise to many space-faring civilizations. Surely a few of these space-faring civilizations would be inclined to explore, to colonize nearby stars, to multiply and spread out. Because the galaxy is a "mere" 10^5 light years across, it would take such a civilization just a few million years to visit every single star system it contains, even traveling at a fraction of the speed of light. Yet there is no convincing evidence that Earth has ever been visited by extraterrestrial explorers or colonists. "So where is everybody?" Fermi asked.

There are many possible answers to Fermi's paradox, too many to enumerate here. But according to one sort of answer, the reason we haven't encountered extraterrestrial intelligence is that every advanced civilization destroys itself when its technology reaches a certain level. This would be a disturbing answer if it were true, because it would imply that this cataclysm, this *great filter* as economist Robin Hanson calls it, lies ahead of us.[17] But what could it be, this great filter? Could it be nuclear war? Could it be an abuse of biotechnology, or an accident with nanotechnology? Or could it, perhaps, be the creation of hostile artificial intelligence?

Perhaps technological development always follows a similar path for every civilization, everywhere in the galaxy. When a civilization's technology reaches a certain level, it becomes easy to engineer a self-improving artificial general intelligence. Yet, at that point, the obstacles to making it safe remain insurmountable. Even if the danger is widely understood, someone (some blob, some hive, or whatever) somewhere on the planet in question is bound to make one. After that, everything is paperclips, so to speak. All is lost.

Then again, if we follow this alarmist argument through to its conclusion, we should expect the extraterrestrial AIs (rather than the extraterrestrials themselves) to multiply and spread out. That was the culmination of Bostrom's paperclip maximizer thought experiment. They would do this, not through some innate urge to explore or to increase in number but in order to maximize their reward function, whatever that might be, the assumption being that the mathematics underlying the design of AIs is the same everywhere. So, to reframe Fermi's question in Bostrom's terms, why aren't we all paperclips? Or, less fancifully, why aren't we all computronium? The fact that we are not is reassuring, but it re-opens the question of our place in the cosmos.

If we are alone, for whatever reason, and if machine superintelligence is possible, then what an enormous responsibility we have. We must decide what to do with the technology, not just for the sake of humanity but to make a future for consciousness itself in this galaxy. As for the human species, the hope is that artificial intelligence, far from destroying us, will help us realize our boldest aspirations while pursuing our highest ideals. For my part, as I watch a wren through the kitchen window, clinging to a hawthorn bush, I hope we never lose sight of the things we already have that still matter, whatever the future holds.

GLOSSARY

Artificial general intelligence (AGI)
Artificial intelligence that is not specialized to carry out specific tasks, but can learn to perform as broad a range of tasks as a human. The term has been popularized by Ben Goertzel.

Big data
In the context of artificial intelligence, a catch-all term to denote quantities of data so large (e.g., billions of training examples) that they enable the performance of tasks (e.g., machine translation) that were not possible with smaller datasets (e.g., comprising only millions of training examples).

Cognitive enhancement
The use of technology, such as drugs or neural prosthesis, to amplify intelligence.

Common sense
In the context of artificial intelligence, a sufficient understanding of the everyday physical and social world to enable the consequences of commonplace actions to be foreseen. In this sense it is seen to be a prerequisite of artificial general intelligence.

Computronium
A hypothetical material capable of performing the maximum amount of computation that is theoretically possible in matter.

Convergent instrumental goals
Goals that indirectly subserve an AI's reward function, and are likely to do so regardless of what that reward function is. Examples include self-preservation and the acquisition of resources.

Deep learning
A machine learning technique that involves multiple, hierarchically organized layers of artificial neurons.

Embodiment
In the context of an AI system, being in control of a spatially located body with sensory and motor apparatus. This might be a physical body (i.e., the human body or a robot body) or a virtual body (in a computer simulation).

Existential risk
Any eventuality, either natural or human-made, that is capable of extinguishing the human species or permanently curbing its potential. The development of recursively self-improving artificial intelligence could be regarded as an existential risk.

Exponential
A mathematical function whose rate of increase at any given time depends on the value of the function at that time. Moore's law is the classic example of an exponential technological trend.

Fermi's paradox
The puzzle, first articulated by Enrico Fermi, that our planet seems never to have been visited by extraterrestrials despite the fact that there has been ample time for any sufficiently advanced extraterrestrial civilization to have spread throughout the galaxy.

Friendly AI
Artificial intelligence of human level or beyond that is guaranteed to have a positive effect on humanity, and not to pose an existential risk. The term was coined by Eliezer Yudkowsky.

Great filter
In the context of Fermi's paradox, the hypothesized cause for the demise of any sufficiently advanced extraterrestrial civilization before it has a chance to spread throughout the galaxy. The development of hostile machine superintelligence is one candidate. The term was coined by Robin Hanson.

Human-level AI
An artificial intelligence capable of matching humans in every (or nearly every) sphere of intellectual activity.

Intelligence explosion
A very rapid increase in intelligence resulting from uncontrolled feedback in a recursively self-improving artificial intelligence. This would yield machine superintelligence.

Law of accelerating returns
A principle governing certain kinds of technological progress wherein improvements in a technology enable that technology to improve more rapidly. Moore's law is an example.

Machine consciousness
Weakly construed, the possession by an artificial intelligence of a set of cognitive attributes that are associated with consciousness in humans, such as awareness, self-awareness, or cognitive integration. Strongly construed, the possession by an AI of properly phenomenological states, perhaps entailing the capacity for suffering.

Mind uploading
The hypothetical transfer of a human mind from its original biological substrate to a computational substrate, by means of whole brain emulation, for example. On the assumption that the person survives the process, this is a potential route to indefinite life extension.

Moore's law
The observation/prediction, first made by Intel's Gordon Moore, that the number of transistors that can be fabricated on a given area of silicon doubles roughly every eighteen months.

Optimization
The computational process of finding a mathematical structure that maximizes a given utility function or reward function. Many cognitive operations can be cast as optimization problems.

Oracle AI
A form of artificial intelligence that doesn't act directly on the world, but that only answers questions. Constructing only oracle AIs is one way to mitigate the risks of superintelligence.

Paperclip maximizer
A hypothetical AI system that features in a thought experiment of Nick Bostrom used to illustrate one way in which a superintelligent machine could fail catastrophically (by filling the world with paperclip factories).

Quantum computer
A computer that exploits quantum effects to achieve high performance. Quantum computers may (or may not) accelerate progress toward AI at human level and beyond.

Recursive self-improvement
The amplification of intelligence in an AI system that can rewrite its own code and/or redesign its own hardware to be better. The rate of self-improvement is potentially subject to the "law of accelerating returns," which means that a recursively self-improving AI could cause an intelligence explosion.

Reinforcement learning
A branch of machine learning that concerns the acquisition, through trial and error, of a policy for action that maximizes expected future reward.

Reward function
In the context of reinforcement learning or optimization, the function that is being maximized. Also called a utility function or (if minimized rather than maximized) a cost function.

Seed AI
The first AI in a series of recursively self-improving systems. Ensuring that the seed AI has the right properties, including the right initial reward function, could be vital to guaranteeing safety in the event of an intelligence explosion.

Superintelligence
Artificial intelligence that can outwit humans in every (or almost every) intellectual sphere

Technological singularity
The prospective development of human-level artificial intelligence, rapidly followed by the arrival of superhuman-level artificial intelligence, precipitating an unprecedented level of social change. This sense of the term is due to Vernor Vinge (1993). Ray Kurzweil (2005) uses the term "singularity" somewhat differently, to mean the (predicted) moment in history when the totality of non-biological intelligence on the planet exceeds the totality of human intelligence.

Transhumanism
A movement dedicated to enabling humans to transcend biological limitations, for example, by greatly extending lifespans or through cognitive enhancement.

Turing machine
An idealized mathematical description of a digital computer proposed by Alan Turing. Theoretically speaking, all digital computers are Turing machines.

Turing Test
A test for intelligence inspired by Alan Turing that involves a judge and two players, one human and one a computer. The judge engages in a conversation with the two players, not knowing which is which. If the judge is unable to tell which is the human and which is the machine, then the machine is said to pass the Turing Test.

Universal artificial intelligence
An idealized mathematical model of perfect artificial intelligence, proposed by Marcus Hutter, that combines reinforcement learning and probabilistic model building.

Vicarious embodiment
The ability of an AI to learn from a massive repository of other embodied agents' recorded interactions with the world as much as if the AI were embodied itself.

Whole brain emulation (WBE)
The process of making an exact computer-simulated copy of the brain of a particular animal (e.g., a particular human). The term was coined Randal Koene.

Zombie AI
A hypothetical artificial intelligence that can perfectly mimic the behavior of a conscious being although it has no phenomenal consciousness.

NOTES

Introduction

1. The first use of the term "singularity" in roughly this way is attributed to von Neumann (S. Ulam, 1958, "John von Neumann 1903–1957." *Bulletin of the American Mathematical Society* 64 93, part 20, 1–49). The term was popularized by Kurzweil in his 2005 book *The Singularity is Near*. Several senses of the term have currency today. The one assumed in this book is closest to that of Vinge in his 1993 essay "The Coming Technological Singularity."

2. G. E. Moore (1965), "Cramming More Components onto Integrated Circuits," *Electronics* (April 19): 114–17.

3. See Kurzweil (2005). Although Kurzweil's book dates from 2005, the exponential trends he identifies (e.g., Moore's law) remain valid ten years on.

4. Kurzweil (2005), p.19. See also J. Schmidhuber (2007), "New Millennium AI and the Convergence of History," in W. Duch and J. Mandziuk (eds.), *Challenges to Computational Intelligence*, Springer, 15–35.

Chapter 1

1. A. M. Turing (1950), "Computing Machinery and Intelligence," *Mind* 49 (236): 433–60.

2. Quoted in J. L. Casti (1988), *The Cambridge Quintet: A Work of Scientific Speculation* (Perseus Books), 180.

3. The term "artificial general intelligence" has recently gained currency thanks to independent AI researcher Ben Goertzel. But the problem was recognized long ago, not least by the field's founders; see J. McCarthy (1987), "Generality in Artificial Intelligence," *Communications of the ACM* 30 (12): 1030–35.

4. A. A. S. Weir, J. Chappell, and A. Kacelnik (2002), "Shaping of Hooks in New Caledonian Crows," *Science* 297: 981.

5. The term "whole brain emulation" was coined by neuroscientist Randal Koene.

Chapter 2

1. See A. Sandberg and N. Bostrom (2008), "Whole Brain Emulation: A Road-map," Technical Report 2008-3, Future of Humanity Institute, Oxford.

2. M. Ahrens and P. J. Keller (2013), "Whole-Brain Functional Imaging at Cellular Resolution Using Light-Sheet Microscopy," *Nature Methods* 10: 413–20.

3. A. M. Zador et al. (2012), "Sequencing the Connectome," *PLoS Biology* 10 (10): e1001411.

4. For a related proposal, see D. Seo et al. (2013), "Neural Dust: An Ultrasonic, Low Power Solution for Chronic Brain Machine Interfaces," http://arxiv.org/abs/1307.2196.

5. This is roughly the approach taken by the ten-year EU funded *Human Brain Project*, begun in 2013.

6. Mathematically speaking, the physical properties of actual neurons cannot be perfectly represented in a conventional digital computer because they are analog quantities. (Hence the scare quotes in the previous paragraph.)

7. Carver Mead set out the principles of neuromorphic engineering in the 1980s. For a recent review, see G. Indiveri et al. (2011), "Neuromorphic Silicon Neuron Circuits," *Frontiers in Neuroscience* 5: art. 73. The promising idea of 3D-printed neuromorphic hardware is discussed in A.D.Maynard (2014), "Could We 3D Print an Artificial Mind?" *Nature Nanotechnology* 9: 955–56.

8. In *The Emperor's New Mind: Concerning Computers, Minds and The Laws of Physics* (Oxford University Press, 1989), physicist Roger Penrose claims that consciousness and intelligence in the human mind depend on certain quantum phenomena in the brain. If he were right, then effective indistinguishability would not be possible for whole brain emulation using classical (digital) computation. However, few neuroscientists support his views. Either way, the issue is orthogonal to the present one of parallelism.

9. C. S. Lent, B. Isaksen, and M. Lieberman (2003), "Molecular Quantum-Dot Cellular Automata," *Journal American Chemical Society* 125: 1056–63.

10. S. Lloyd (2000), "Ultimate Physical Limits to Computation," *Nature* 406: 1047–54.

11. The feasibility of cognitive prostheses has been demonstrated by Theodore Berger and colleagues; see T. W. Berger et al. (2011), "A Cortical Neural Prosthesis for Restoring and Enhancing Memory," *Journal of Neural Engineering* 8 (4): 046017.

Chapter 3

1. A. Halevy, P. Norvig, and F. Pereira (2009), "The Unreasonable Effectiveness of Data," *IEEE Intelligent Systems* (March–April): 8–12.

2. M. Hutter (2005), *Universal Artificial Intelligence: Sequential Decisions Based on Algorithmic Probability* (Springer). For a more digestible and

up-to-date overview, see M. Hutter (2012), "One Decade of Universal Artificial Intelligence," http://arxiv.org/abs/1202.6153.

3. A mid-2010s AI system that roughly conforms to this blueprint is Google DeepMind's DQN. See V. Mnih,et al. (2015), "Human-Level Control through Deep Reinforcement Learning," *Nature* 518: 529–33.

Chapter 4

1. The possibility of an intelligence explosion was first mooted in the 1960s by the computer scientist Jack Good (also a wartime code-breaker who worked with Turing); see I. J. Good (1965), "Speculations Concerning the First Ultra-intelligent Machine," in F. L. Alt and M. Rubinoff (eds.), *Advances in Computers* 6: 31–88. The potential ramifications of an intelligence explosion are explored in depth in Nick Bostrom's book *Superintelligence: Paths, Dangers, Strategies* (Oxford Univeristy Press, 2014).

2. This is the point of John Searle's controversial *Chinese room argument* (J. R. Searle, 1980, "Minds, Brains, and Programs," *Behavioral and Brain Sciences* 3: 417–58). Whatever the merits of his argument, its conclusion—that under-standing doesn't result from the mere manipulation of symbols—resonates with the present discussion of engineered AI. However, it has less appeal in the context of human-like, brain-based AI.

Chapter 5

1. For example, see E. Thompson (2007), *Mind in Life: Biology, Phenomenology, and the Sciences of Mind* (Belknap Harvard).

2. For example, see D. Dennett (1991), *Consciousness Explained* (Penguin).

3. See chapter 7 of D. J. Chalmers (1996), *The Conscious Mind: In Search of a Fundamental Theory* (Oxford University Press).

4. B. J. Baars (1988), *A Cognitive Theory of Consciousness* (Cambridge University Press); G. Tononi (2008), "Consciousness as Integrated Information: a Provisional Manifesto," *Biological Bulletin* 215: 216–42. For more on global workspace theory, see Shanahan (2010) and S. Dehaene et al. (2014), "Toward a Computational Theory of Conscious Processing," *Current Opinion in Neurobiology* 25: 76–84.

5. According to philosopher Thomas Metzinger, attempts to create machine consciousness should be banned; see T. Metzinger (2003), *Being No-One: The Self-Model Theory of Subjectivity* (MIT Press), pp.620–22.

6. D. J. Chalmers (1996), *The Conscious Mind: In Search of a Fundamental Theory* (Oxford University Press). For a critique of this distinction, see chapter 1 of Shanahan (2010).

7. T. Nagel (1974), "What Is It Like to Be a Bat?" *Philosophical Review* 83 (4): 435–50.

8. See chapter 9 of *The Principles of Psychology* (1890).

9. For a related discussion, see M. Shanahan (2012), "Satori before Singularity," *Journal of Consciousness Studies* 19 (7–8): 87–102.

Chapter 6

1. H. Moravec (1999), 164–65.

2. This section is based on Kurzweil's *The Singularity Is Near* (Viking, 2005).

3. See Palyanov et al. (2012), "Towards a Virtual *C. elegans*: A Framework for Simulation and Visualization of the Neuromuscular System in a 3D Environment," *In Silico Biology* 11: 137–47.

4. F. Nietzsche (1881), *Daybreak*, bk. 5.

5. For a more detailed treatment of the issues in this section, see Brynjolfsson and McAfee (2014).

6. J. Lanier (2013), *Who Owns the Future?* (Alan Lane).

Chapter 7

1. There isn't space here to represent the broad set of views that fall under the umbrella of transhumanism. See M. More and N. Vita-More (2013).

2. F. Fukuyama (2004), Transhumansim, *Foreign Policy* 144: 42–43.

3. Fukuyama (2002), p. 172.

4. Ibid., p.173.

5. F. Nietzsche (1883), *Thus Spoke Zarathustra*, Prologue 4.

6. The discussion of personal identity here draws on D. Chalmers (2010) as well as chapter 10 of D. Parfit (1984), *Reasons and Persons* (Oxford University Press).

7. For further discussion of this issue, see Yudkowsky (2008) and Bostrom (2014).

8. Yudkowsky suggests a sophisticated strategy along these lines, based on what he calls *coherent extrapolated volition*; see E. Yudkowsky (2004), "Coherent Extrapolated Volition," The Singularity Institute, http://intelligence.org/files/CEV.pdf. See also chapter 13 of Bostrom (2014).

9. Bostrom (2014), p. 123.

10. See also S. Omohundro (2008), "The Basic AI Drives," in P. Wang, B. Goertzel, and S. Franklin (eds.), *Proceedings of the 1st AGI Conference*, 483–92.

11. Yudkowsky (2008), p. 333.

12. K. E. Drexler (1986), *Engines of Creation: The Coming Era of Nanotechnology* (Anchor Books), chapter 11.

13. The second law is "A robot must obey the orders given to it by human beings, except where such orders would conflict with the first law" and the third law is "A robot must protect its own existence as long as such protection does not conflict with the first or second law."

14. Dilemmas of this sort are familiar to moral philosophers, who call them "trolley problems" after a thought experiment of Philippa Foot.

15. See Geraci (2010).

16. E. M. Jones (1985), "'Where Is Everybody?' An Account of Fermi's Question," *Physics Today* 38 (8): 11–13.

17. R. Hanson (1998), "The Great Filter—Are We Almost Past It?" http://hanson.gmu.edu/greatfilter.html.

FURTHER READINGS

Barrat, J. 2013. Our Final Invention: Artificial Intelligence and the End of the Human Era. Thomas Dunne Books.

Blackford, R., and D. Broderick, eds. 2014. Intelligence Unbound: The Future of Uploaded and Machine Minds. Wiley Blackwell.

Bostrom, N. 2014. Superintelligence: Paths, Dangers, Strategies. Oxford University Press.

Brynjolfsson, E., and A. McAfee. 2014. The Second Machine Age: Work, Progress, and Prosperity in a Time of Brilliant Technologies. Norton.

Chalmers, D. 2010. "The Singularity: A Philosophical Analysis." *Journal of Consciousness Studies* 17 (9–10): 7–65.

Eden, A. H., J. H. Moor, and J. H. Soraker, eds. 2013. Singularity Hypotheses: A Scientific and Philosophical Assessment. Springer.

Fukuyama, F. 2002. Our Posthuman Future: Consequences of the Biotechnology Revolution. Profile Books.

Geraci, R. 2010. Apocalyptic AI: Visions of Heaven in Robotics, Artificial Intelligence, and Virtual Reality. Oxford University Press.

Good, I. J. 1965. "Speculations Concerning the First Ultraintelligent Machine." In Advances in Computers 6, ed. F. L. Alt and M. Rubinoff, 31–88. Academic Press.

Joy, B. 2000. "Why the Future Doesn't Need Us." *Wired* 8.04.

Kurzweil, R. 2005. The Singularity Is Near. Viking.

Moravec, H. 1999. Robot: Mere Machine to Transcendent Mind. Oxford University Press.

More, M., and N. Vita-More, eds. 2013. *The Transhumanist Reader: Classical and Contemporary Essays on the Science, Technology, and Philosophy of the Human Future*. Wiley Blackwell.

Shanahan, M. 2010. Embodiment and the Inner Life: Cognition and Consciousness in the Space of Possible Minds. Oxford University Press.

Vinge, V. 1993. "The Coming Technological Singularity: How to Survive in the Post-Human Era." In *Vision-21: Interdisciplinary Science and Engineering in the Era of Cyberspace*, 11–22. NASA Conference Publication 10129. NASA Lewis Research Center.

Yudkowsky, E. 2008. "Artificial Intelligence as a Positive and Negative Factor in Global Risk." In Global Catastrophic Risks, ed. N. Bostrom and M. M. Cirkovic, 308–45. Oxford University Press.

INDEX